Great Military Commanders

George S Patton

A Biography

Compiled by

Nevaeh Melancon

Scribbles

Year of Publication 2018

ISBN : 9789352979400

Book Published by

Scribbles

(An Imprint of Alpha Editions)

email - alphaedis@gmail.com

Produced by: PediaPress GmbH
Limburg an der Lahn
Germany
http://pediapress.com/

Contents

Patton

George S. Patton

General
George S. Patton

Patton as a lieutenant general

Birth name	George Smith Patton Jr.
Nickname(s)	"Bandito" "Old Blood and Guts"
Born	November 11, 1885 San Gabriel, California, U.S.
Died	December 21, 1945 (aged 60) Heidelberg, Germany
Buried	American Cemetery and Memorial, Luxembourg City
Allegiance	United States of America
Service/-<wbr/>>branch	United States Army

1

Years of service	1909–1945
Rank	General
Unit	Cavalry Branch
Commands held	Seventh United States Army Third United States Army Fifteenth United States Army *See other commands* 304th Tank Brigade 3rd Squadron, 3rd Cavalry 5th Cavalry Regiment 3d Cavalry Regiment 2nd Brigade, 2nd Armored Division 2nd Armored Division I Armored Corps Desert Training Center II Corps
Battles/-wars	*See battles* **Mexican Revolution** • Battle of San Miguelito **World War I** • Saint Mihiel Campaign • Meuse-Argonne Campaign **World War II** • Operation Torch • North African Campaign • Tunisia Campaign • Sicily Campaign • Lorraine Campaign • Ardennes Campaign • Rhineland Campaign • Central Europe Campaign
Awards	Distinguished Service Cross (2) Distinguished Service Medal (3) Silver Star (2) Legion of Merit Bronze Star Purple Heart *Complete list of decorations*
Relations	George Patton IV (son) John K. Waters (son-in-law)
Signature	*G S Patton Jr.*

George Smith Patton Jr. (November 11, 1885 – December 21, 1945) was a General of the United States Army who commanded the U.S. Seventh Army in the Mediterranean theater of World War II, and the U.S. Third Army in France and Germany following the Allied invasion of Normandy in June 1944.

Born in 1885 to a family with an extensive military background that spanned both the United States and Confederate States armies, Patton attended the Virginia Military Institute and the U.S. Military Academy at West Point. He studied fencing and designed the M1913 Cavalry Saber, more commonly known as the "Patton Sword", and was sufficiently skilled in the sport to compete in the 1912 Summer Olympics in Stockholm, Sweden.

Patton first saw combat during the Pancho Villa Expedition in 1916, taking part in America's first military action using motor vehicles. As part of the newly formed United States Tank Corps of the American Expeditionary Forces he saw action in World War I, commanding the U.S. tank school in France before being wounded while leading tanks into combat near the end of the war. In the interwar period, Patton remained a central figure in the development of the Army's armored warfare doctrine, serving in numerous staff positions throughout the country. Rising through the ranks, he commanded the 2nd Armored Division at the time of the American entry into World War II.

Patton led U.S. troops into the Mediterranean theater with an invasion of Casablanca during Operation Torch in 1942, where he later established himself as an effective commander through his rapid rehabilitation of the demoralized U.S. II Corps. He commanded the U.S. Seventh Army during the Allied invasion of Sicily, where he was the first Allied commander to reach Messina. There he was embroiled in controversy after he slapped two shell-shocked soldiers under his command, and was temporarily removed from battlefield command. He then was assigned a key role in Operation Fortitude, the Allies' disinformation campaign for Operation Overlord. Following the invasion of Normandy in June 1944, Patton was given command of the Third Army, which conducted a highly successful rapid armored drive across France. Under his decisive leadership the Third Army took the lead in relieving beleaguered American troops at Bastogne during the Battle of the Bulge, after which his forces drove deep into Nazi Germany by the end of the war.

During the Allied occupation of Germany Patton was named military governor of Bavaria, but was relieved over his aggressive statements towards the Soviet Union and trivializing denazification. He commanded the United States Fifteenth Army for slightly more than two months. Severely injured in an auto accident, he died in Germany twelve days later, on December 21, 1945.

Patton's colorful image, hard-driving personality and success as a commander were at times overshadowed by his controversial public statements. His philosophy of leading from the front and ability to inspire troops with attention-getting, vulgarity-ridden speeches, such as a famous address to the Third Army, met with mixed receptions, favorably with his troops but much less so among a sharply divided Allied high command. His strong emphasis on rapid and aggressive offensive action proved effective, and he was regarded highly by his opponents in the German High Command. An award-winning biographical film released in 1970, *Patton*, helped solidify his image as an American folk hero.

Figure 1: *Anne Wilson "Nita" Patton, Patton's sister. She was engaged to John J. Pershing in 1917–18.*

Early life

George Smith Patton Jr. was born on November 11, 1885[1,2] in San Gabriel, California, to George Smith Patton Sr. and his wife Ruth Wilson. Patton had a younger sister, Anne, who was nicknamed "Nita."[3]

As a child Patton had difficulty learning to read and write, but eventually overcame this and was known in his adult life to be an avid reader.[4]</ref> He was tutored from home until the age of eleven, when he was enrolled in Stephen Clark's School for Boys, a private school in Pasadena, for six years. Patton was described as an intelligent boy and was widely read on classical military history, particularly the exploits of Hannibal, Scipio Africanus, Julius Caesar, Joan of Arc, and Napoleon Bonaparte, as well as those of family friend John Singleton Mosby, who frequently stopped by the Patton family home when George S. Patton was a child.[3] He was also a devoted horseback rider.[5]

Patton married Beatrice Banning Ayer, the daughter of Boston industrialist Frederick Ayer, on May 26, 1910, in Beverly Farms, Massachusetts. They had three children, Beatrice Smith (born March 1911), Ruth Ellen (born February 1915), and George Patton IV (born December 1923).[6]

Patton never seriously considered a career other than the military.[5] At the age of seventeen he sought an appointment to the United States Military Academy.

Figure 2: *Patton at the Virginia Military Institute, 1907*

Patton applied to several universities with Reserve Officer's Training Corps programs. Patton was accepted to Princeton College but eventually decided on VMI, which his father and grandfather had attended.[7] He attended the school from 1903 to 1904 and, though he struggled with reading and writing, performed exceptionally in uniform and appearance inspection as well as military drill. While Patton was at VMI, a senator from California nominated him for West Point.[8]

In his plebe (first) year at West Point, Patton adjusted easily to the routine. However, his academic performance was so poor that he was forced to repeat his first year after failing mathematics.[9] Patton excelled at military drills though his academic performance remained average. He was cadet sergeant major during his junior year, and the cadet adjutant his senior year. He also joined the football team, but he injured his arm and stopped playing on several occasions. Instead he tried out for the sword team and track and field and specialized in the modern pentathlon,[10]. He competed in this sport in the 1912 Summer Olympics in Stockholm, and he finished in fifth place - right behind four Swedes.[11]

Patton was ranked #46 out of 103 cadets at West Point, and he graduated on June 11, 1909, and was commissioned as a second lieutenant in the Cavalry Branch of the United States Army.[12,13]

Ancestry

The Patton family was of Irish, Scots-Irish, English, Scottish, and Welsh ancestry. His great-grandmother came from an aristocratic Welsh family, descended from many Welsh lords of Glamorgan,[5] which had an extensive military background. Patton believed he had former lives as a soldier and took pride in mystical ties with his ancestors. Though not directly descended from George Washington, Patton traced some of his English colonial roots to George Washington's great-grandfather.[14] He was also descended from England's King Edward I through Edward's son Edmund of Woodstock, 1st Earl of Kent.[14] Family belief held the Pattons were descended from sixteen barons who had signed the Magna Carta.[14] Patton believed in reincarnation, and his ancestry was very important to him, forming a central part of his personal identity.[15] The first Patton in America was Robert Patton, born in Ayr, Scotland. He emigrated to Culpeper, Virginia, from Glasgow, in either 1769 or 1770.[16] His paternal grandfather was George Smith Patton, who commanded the 22nd Virginia Infantry under Jubal Early in the Civil War and was killed in the Third Battle of Winchester, while his great-uncle Waller T. Patton was killed in Pickett's Charge during the Battle of Gettysburg. Patton also descended from Hugh Mercer, who had been killed in the Battle of Princeton during the American Revolution. Patton's father, who graduated from the Virginia Military Institute (VMI), became a lawyer and later the district attorney of Los Angeles County. Patton's maternal grandfather was Benjamin Davis Wilson, a merchant who had been the second Mayor of Los Angeles. His father was a wealthy rancher and lawyer who owned a thousand-acre ranch near Pasadena, California.[17] Patton is also a descendant of French Huguenot Louis DuBois.[18,19]

Junior officer

Patton's first posting was with the 15th Cavalry at Fort Sheridan, Illinois,[20] where he established himself as a hard-driving leader who impressed superiors with his dedication.[21] In late 1911, Patton was transferred to Fort Myer, Virginia, where many of the Army's senior leaders were stationed. Befriending Secretary of War Henry L. Stimson, Patton served as his aide at social functions on top of his regular duties as quartermaster for his troop.[22]

1912 Olympics

For his skill with running and fencing, Patton was selected as the Army's entry for the first modern pentathlon at the 1912 Olympic Games in Stockholm, Sweden.[23] Of 42 competitors, Patton placed twenty-first on the pistol range,

Figure 3: *Patton on his steeplechase horse, Wooltex, in 1914*

seventh in swimming, fourth in fencing, sixth in the equestrian competition, and third in the footrace, finishing fifth overall and first among the non-Swedish competitors.[24] There was some controversy concerning his performance in the pistol shooting competition, where he used a .38 caliber pistol while most of the other competitors chose .22 caliber firearms. He claimed that the holes in the paper from his early shots were so large that some of his later bullets passed through them, but the judges decided he missed the target completely once. Modern competitions on this level frequently now employ a moving background to specifically track multiple shots through the same hole.[25,26] If his assertion was correct, Patton would likely have won an Olympic medal in the event.[27] The judges' ruling was upheld. Patton's only comment on the matter was:

<templatestyles src="Template:Quote/styles.css"/>

> *The high spirit of sportsmanship and generosity manifested throughout speaks volumes for the character of the officers of the present day. There was not a single incident of a protest or any unsportsmanlike quibbling or fighting for points which I may say, marred some of the other civilian competitions at the Olympic Games. Each man did his best and took what fortune sent them like a true soldier, and at the end we all felt more like good friends and comrades than rivals in a severe competition, yet this*

spirit of friendship in no manner detracted from the zeal with which all
strove for success.[25]

Sword design

Following the 1912 Olympics, Patton traveled to Saumur, France, where he learned fencing techniques from Adjutant Charles Cléry, a French "master of arms" and instructor of fencing at the cavalry school there.[28] Bringing these lessons back to Fort Myer, Patton redesigned saber combat doctrine for the U.S. cavalry, favoring thrusting attacks over the standard slashing maneuver and designing a new sword for such attacks. He was temporarily assigned to the Office of the Army Chief of Staff, and in 1913, the first 20,000 of the Model 1913 Cavalry Saber—popularly known as the "Patton sword"—were ordered. Patton then returned to Saumur to learn advanced techniques before bringing his skills to the Mounted Service School at Fort Riley, Kansas, where he would be both a student and a fencing instructor. He was the first Army officer to be designated "Master of the Sword",[29,30] a title denoting the school's top instructor in swordsmanship.[31] Arriving in September 1913, he taught fencing to other cavalry officers, many of whom were senior to him in rank.[32] Patton graduated from this school in June 1915. He was originally intended to return to the 15th Cavalry,[33] which was bound for the Philippines. Fearing this assignment would dead-end his career, Patton traveled to Washington, D.C. during 11 days of leave and convinced influential friends to arrange a reassignment for him to the 8th Cavalry at Fort Bliss, Texas, anticipating that instability in Mexico might boil over into a full-scale civil war.[34] In the meantime, Patton was selected to participate in the 1916 Summer Olympics, but that olympiad was cancelled due to World War I.[35]

Pancho Villa Expedition

In 1915 Patton was assigned to border patrol duty with A Troop of the 8th Cavalry, based in Sierra Blanca.[37,38] During his time in the town, Patton took to wearing his M1911 Colt .45 in his belt rather than a holster. His firearm discharged accidentally one night in a saloon, so he swapped it for an ivory-handled Colt Single Action Army revolver, a weapon that would later become an icon of Patton's image.[39]

In March 1916 Mexican forces loyal to Pancho Villa crossed into New Mexico and raided the border town of Columbus. The violence in Columbus killed several Americans. In response, the U.S. launched the Pancho Villa Expedition into Mexico. Chagrined to discover that his unit would not participate, Patton appealed to expedition commander John J. Pershing, and was named his personal aide for the expedition. This meant that Patton would have some

Figure 4: *The durability of the 1915 Dodge Brothers Model 30-35 touring car won renown for the new automaker following its use in the 1916 Pancho Villa Expedition*[36]

role in organizing the effort, and his eagerness and dedication to the task impressed Pershing.[40,41] Patton modeled much of his leadership style after Pershing, who favored strong, decisive actions and commanding from the front.[42,43] As an aide, Patton oversaw the logistics of Pershing's transportation and acted as his personal courier.[44]

In mid-April, Patton asked Pershing for the opportunity to command troops, and was assigned to Troop C of the 13th Cavalry to assist in the manhunt for Villa and his subordinates.[45] His initial combat experience came on May 14, 1916 in what would become the first motorized attack in the history of U.S. warfare. A force under his command of ten soldiers and two civilian guides with the 6th Infantry in three Dodge touring cars surprised three of Villa's men during a foraging expedition, killing Julio Cárdenas and two of his guards.[41,46] It was not clear if Patton personally killed any of the men, but he was known to have wounded all three.[47] The incident garnered Patton both Pershing's good favor and widespread media attention as a "bandit killer".[41,48] Shortly after, he was promoted to first lieutenant while a part of the 10th Cavalry on May 23, 1916.[37] Patton remained in Mexico until the end of the year. President Woodrow Wilson forbade the expedition from conducting aggressive patrols deeper into Mexico, so it remained encamped in the Mexican border states for much of that time. In October Patton briefly retired to California after

Figure 5: *Patton at Bourg in France in 1918 with a Renault FT light tank*

being burned by an exploding gas lamp.[49] He returned from the expedition permanently in February 1917.[50]

World War I

After the Villa Expedition, Patton was detailed to Front Royal, Virginia, to oversee horse procurement for the Army, but Pershing intervened on his behalf.[50] After the United States entered World War I, and Pershing was named commander of the American Expeditionary Force (AEF) on the Western Front, Patton requested to join his staff.[41] Patton was promoted to captain on May 15, 1917 and left for Europe, among the 180 men of Pershing's advance party which departed May 28 and arrived in Liverpool, England, on June 8.[51] Taken as Pershing's personal aide, Patton oversaw the training of American troops in Paris until September, then moved to Chaumont and assigned as a post adjutant, commanding the headquarters company overseeing the base. Patton was dissatisfied with the post and began to take an interest in tanks, as Pershing sought to give him command of an infantry battalion.[52] While in a hospital for jaundice, Patton met Colonel Fox Conner, who encouraged him to work with tanks instead of infantry.[53]

On November 10, 1917 Patton was assigned to establish the AEF Light Tank School.[41] He left Paris and reported to the French Army's tank training school at Champlieu near Orrouy, where he drove a Renault FT light tank. On November 20, the British launched an offensive towards the important rail center of Cambrai, using an unprecedented number of tanks.[54] At the conclusion of his tour on December 1, Patton went to Albert, 30 miles (48 km) from Cambrai, to be briefed on the results of this attack by the chief of staff of the British Tank Corps, Colonel J. F. C. Fuller.[55] On the way back to Paris, he visited the Renault factory to observe the tanks being manufactured. Patton was promoted to major on January 26, 1918.[53] He received the first ten tanks on March 23, 1918 at the Tank School at Bourg, a small village close to Langres, Haute-Marne département. The only US soldier with tank-driving experience, Patton personally backed seven of the tanks off the train.[56] In the post, Patton trained tank crews to operate in support of infantry, and promoted its acceptance among reluctant infantry officers.[57] He was promoted to lieutenant colonel on April 3, 1918, and attended the Command and General Staff College in Langres.[58]

In August 1918, he was placed in charge of the U.S. 1st Provisional Tank Brigade (redesignated the 304th Tank Brigade on November 6, 1918). Patton's Light Tank Brigade was part of Colonel Samuel Rockenbach's Tank Corps, part of the American First Army.[59] Personally overseeing the logistics of the tanks in their first combat use by U.S. forces, and reconnoitering the target area for their first attack himself, Patton ordered that no U.S. tank be surrendered.[58,60] Patton commanded American-crewed Renault FT tanks at the Battle of Saint-Mihiel,[61] leading the tanks from the front for much of their attack, which began on September 12. He walked in front of the tanks into the German-held village of Essey, and rode on top of a tank during the attack into Pannes, seeking to inspire his men.[62]

Patton's brigade was then moved to support U.S. I Corps in the Meuse-Argonne Offensive on September 26.[61] He personally led a troop of tanks through thick fog as they advanced 5 miles (8 km) into German lines. Around 09:00, Patton was wounded while leading six men and a tank in an attack on German machine guns near the town of Cheppy.[63,64] His orderly, Private First Class Joe Angelo, saved Patton, for which he was later awarded the Distinguished Service Cross.[65] Patton commanded the battle from a shell hole for another hour before being evacuated. He stopped at a rear command post to submit his report before heading to a hospital. Sereno E. Brett, commander of the U.S. 326th Tank Battalion, took command of the brigade in Patton's absence. Patton wrote in a letter to his wife: "The bullet went into the front of my left leg and came out just at the crack of my bottom about two inches to the left of my rectum. It was fired at about 50 m so made a hole about the size of a [silver] dollar where it came out."[66]

Figure 6: *Patton as a temporary colonel at Camp Meade, Maryland, 1919*

While recuperating from his wound, Patton was promoted to colonel in the
Tank Corps of the U.S. National Army on October 17. He returned to duty on
October 28 but saw no further action before hostilities ended with the armistice
of November 11, 1918.[67] For his actions in Cheppy, Patton received the Distinguished Service Cross. For his leadership of the brigade and tank school, he
was awarded the Distinguished Service Medal. He was also awarded the Pur-
ple Heart for his combat wounds after the decoration was created in 1932.[68]

Inter-war years

Patton left France for New York City on March 2, 1919. After the war he
was assigned to Camp Meade, Maryland, and reverted to his permanent rank
of captain on June 30, 1920, though he was promoted to major again the next
day. Patton was given temporary duty in Washington D.C. that year to serve
on a committee writing a manual on tank operations. During this time he developed a belief that tanks should be used not as infantry support, but rather
as an independent fighting force. Patton supported the M1919 tank design
created by J. Walter Christie, a project which was shelved due to financial
considerations.[69] While on duty in Washington, D.C., in 1919, Patton met
Dwight D. Eisenhower,[70] who would play an enormous role in Patton's future

career. During and following Patton's assignment in Hawaii, he and Eisenhower corresponded frequently. Patton sent Eisenhower notes and assistance to help him graduate from the General Staff College.[71] With Christie, Eisenhower, and a handful of other officers, Patton pushed for more development of armored warfare in the interwar era. These thoughts resonated with Secretary of War Dwight Davis, but the limited military budget and prevalence of already-established Infantry and Cavalry branches meant the U.S. would not develop its armored corps much until 1940.[72]

On September 30, 1920, Patton relinquished command of the 304th Tank Brigade and was reassigned to Fort Myer as commander of 3rd Squadron, 3rd Cavalry.[71] Loathing duty as a peacetime staff officer, he spent much time writing technical papers and giving speeches on his combat experiences at the General Staff College.[69] In July 1921 Patton became a member of the American Legion Tank Corps Post No. 19. From 1922 to mid-1923 he attended the Field Officer's Course at the Cavalry School at Fort Riley, then he attended the Command and General Staff College from mid-1923 to mid-1924,[71] graduating 25th out of 248.[73] In August 1923, Patton saved several children from drowning when they fell off a yacht during a boating trip off Salem, Massachusetts. He was awarded the Silver Lifesaving Medal for this action.[74] He was temporarily appointed to the General Staff Corps in Boston, Massachusetts, before being reassigned as G-1 and G-2 of the Hawaiian Division at Schofield Barracks in Honolulu in March 1925.[71]

Patton was made G-3 of the Hawaiian Division for several months, before being transferred in May 1927 to the Office of the Chief of Cavalry in Washington, D.C., where he began to develop the concepts of mechanized warfare. A short-lived experiment to merge infantry, cavalry and artillery into a combined arms force was cancelled after U.S. Congress removed funding. Patton left this office in 1931, returned to Massachusetts and attended the Army War College, becoming a "Distinguished Graduate" in June 1932.[75]

In July 1932, Patton was executive officer of the 3rd Cavalry, which was ordered to Washington by Army Chief of Staff General Douglas MacArthur. Patton took command of the 600 troops of the 3rd Cavalry, and on July 28, MacArthur ordered Patton's troops to advance on protesting veterans known as the "Bonus Army" with tear gas and bayonets. Patton was dissatisfied with MacArthur's conduct, as he recognized the legitimacy of the veterans' complaints and had himself earlier refused to issue the order to employ armed force to disperse the veterans. Patton later stated that, though he found the duty "most distasteful", he also felt that putting the marchers down prevented an insurrection and saved lives and property. He personally led the 3rd Cavalry down Pennsylvania Avenue, dispersing the protesters.[76,77] Patton also encountered his former orderly as one of the marchers and forcibly ordered him away, fearing such a meeting might make the headlines.[78]

Patton was promoted to lieutenant colonel in the regular Army on March 1, 1934, and was transferred to the Hawaiian Division in early 1935 to serve as G-2. Patton followed the growing hostility and conquest aspirations of the militant Japanese leadership. He wrote a plan to intern the Japanese living in the islands in the event of an attack as a result of the atrocities carried out by Japanese soldiers on the Chinese in the Sino-Japanese war. In 1937 he wrote a paper with the title "Surprise" which predicted, with what D'Este termed "chilling accuracy", a surprise attack by the Japanese on Hawaii.[79] Depressed at the lack of prospects for new conflict, Patton took to drinking heavily and allegedly began a brief affair with his 21-year-old niece by marriage, Jean Gordon.[80] This supposed affair distressed his wife and nearly resulted in their separation. Patton's attempts to win her back were said to be among the few instances in which he willingly showed remorse or submission.[81]

Patton continued playing polo and sailing in this time. After sailing back to Los Angeles for extended leave in 1937, he was kicked by a horse and fractured his leg. Patton developed phlebitis from the injury, which nearly killed him. The incident almost forced Patton out of active service, but a six-month administrative assignment in the Academic Department at the Cavalry School at Fort Riley helped him to recover.[80] Patton was promoted to colonel on July 24, 1938 and given command of the 5th Cavalry at Fort Clark, Texas, for six months, a post he relished, but he was reassigned to Fort Myer again in December as commander of the 3rd Cavalry. There, he met Army Chief of Staff George C. Marshall, who was so impressed with him that Marshall considered Patton a prime candidate for promotion to general. In peacetime, though, he would remain a colonel to remain eligible to command a regiment.[82]

Patton had a personal schooner named *When and If*. The schooner was designed by famous naval architect John G. Alden and built in 1939. The schooner's name comes from Patton saying he would sail it "when and if" he returned from war.

World War II

Following the German Army's invasion of Poland and the outbreak of World War II in Europe in September 1939, the U.S. military entered a period of mobilization, and Patton sought to build up the power of U.S. armored forces. During maneuvers the Third Army conducted in 1940, Patton served as an umpire, where he met Adna R. Chaffee Jr. and the two formulated recommendations to develop an armored force. Chaffee was named commander of this force,[83] and created the 1st and 2nd Armored Divisions as well as the first combined arms doctrine. He named Patton commander of the 2nd Armored Brigade, part of the 2nd Armored Division. The division was one of few organized as a heavy formation with many tanks, and Patton was in charge of its training.[84] Patton was promoted to brigadier general on October 2, made acting division commander in November, and on April 4, 1941 was promoted again to major general and made Commanding General (CG) of the 2nd Armored Division.[83] As Chaffee stepped down from command of the I Armored Corps, Patton became the most prominent figure in U.S. armor doctrine. In December 1940, he staged a high-profile mass exercise in which 1,000 tanks and vehicles were driven from Columbus, Georgia, to Panama City, Florida, and back.[85] He repeated the exercise with his entire division of 1,300 vehicles the next month.[86] Patton earned a pilot's license and, during these maneuvers, observed the movements of his vehicles from the air to find ways to deploy them effectively in combat.[85] His exploits earned him a spot on the cover of *Life Magazine*.[87]

Patton led the division during the Tennessee Maneuvers in June 1941, and was lauded for his leadership, executing 48 hours' worth of planned objectives in only nine. During the September Louisiana Maneuvers, his division was part of the losing Red Army in Phase I, but in Phase II was assigned to the Blue Army. His division executed a 400-mile (640 km) end run around the Red Army and "captured" Shreveport, Louisiana. During the October–November Carolina Maneuvers, Patton's division captured Hugh Drum, commander of the opposing army.[88] On January 15, 1942 he was given command of I Armored Corps, and the next month established the Desert Training Center[89] in the Imperial Valley to run training exercises. He commenced these exercises in late 1941 and continued them into the summer of 1942. Patton chose a 10,000-acre (40 km²) expanse of desert area about 50 miles (80 km) southeast of Palm Springs.[90] From his first days as a commander, Patton strongly emphasized the need for armored forces to stay in constant contact with opposing forces. His instinctive preference for offensive movement was typified by an answer Patton gave to war correspondents in a 1944 press conference. In response to a question on whether the Third Army's rapid offensive across France should be slowed to reduce the number of U.S. casualties, Patton replied, "Whenever you slow anything down, you waste human lives."[91] It was around this time that a reporter, after hearing a speech where Patton said that it took "blood and brains" to win in combat, began calling him "blood and guts". The nickname would follow him for the rest of his life.[92] Soldiers under his command were known at times to have quipped, "our blood, his guts". Nonetheless, he was known to be admired widely by the men under his charge.[93]

Figure 7: *Patton (left) with Rear Admiral Henry Kent Hewitt aboard USS Augusta, off the coast of North Africa, November 1942*

North African Campaign

Under Lieutenant General Dwight D. Eisenhower, the Supreme Allied Commander, Patton was assigned to help plan the Allied invasion of French North Africa as part of Operation Torch in the summer of 1942.[94,95] Patton commanded the Western Task Force, consisting of 33,000 men in 100 ships, in landings centered on Casablanca, Morocco. The landings, which took place on November 8, 1942, were opposed by Vichy French forces, but Patton's men quickly gained a beachhead and pushed through fierce resistance. Casablanca fell on November 11 and Patton negotiated an armistice with French General Charles Noguès.[96,97] The Sultan of Morocco was so impressed that he presented Patton with the Order of Ouissam Alaouite, with the citation *"Les Lions dans leurs tanières tremblent en le voyant approcher"* (The lions in their dens tremble at his approach).[98] Patton oversaw the conversion of Casablanca into a military port and hosted the Casablanca Conference in January 1943.[99]

On March 6, 1943, following the defeat of the U.S. II Corps by the German Afrika Korps, commanded by *Generalfeldmarschall* Erwin Rommel, at the Battle of Kasserine Pass, Patton replaced Major General Lloyd Fredendall as Commanding General of the II Corps and was promoted to lieutenant general. Soon thereafter, he had Major General Omar Bradley reassigned to his corps as its deputy commander.[100] With orders to take the battered and demoralized formation into action in 10 days' time, Patton immediately introduced sweeping changes, ordering all soldiers to wear clean, pressed and complete uniforms, establishing rigorous schedules, and requiring strict adherence to military protocol. He continuously moved throughout the command talking with men, seeking to shape them into effective soldiers. He pushed them hard, and sought to reward them well for their accomplishments.[101] His uncompromising leadership style is evidenced by his orders for an attack on a hill position near Gafsa which are reported to have ended "I expect to see such casualties among officers, particularly staff officers, as will convince me that a serious effort has been made to capture this objective."[102]

Patton's training was effective, and on March 17, the U.S. 1st Infantry Division took Gafsa, winning the Battle of El Guettar, and pushing a German and Italian armored force back twice. In the meantime, on April 5, he removed Major General Orlando Ward, commanding the 1st Armored Division, after its lackluster performance at Maknassy against numerically inferior German forces. Advancing on Gabès, Patton's corps pressured the Mareth Line.[101] During this time, he reported to British General Sir Harold Alexander, commander of the 18th Army Group, and came into conflict with Air Vice Marshal Sir Arthur Coningham about the lack of close air support being provided for his troops. When Coningham dispatched three officers to Patton's headquarters to persuade him that the British were providing ample air support, they came under German air attack mid-meeting, and part of the ceiling of Patton's office collapsed around them. Speaking later of the German pilots who had struck, Patton remarked, "if I could find the sons of bitches who flew those planes, I'd mail each of them a medal."[103] By the time his force reached Gabès, the Germans had abandoned it. He then relinquished command of II Corps to Bradley, and returned to the I Armored Corps in Casablanca to help plan Operation Husky, the Allied invasion of Sicily. Fearing U.S. troops would be sidelined, he convinced British commanders to allow them to continue fighting through to the end of the Tunisia Campaign before leaving on this new assignment.[103,104]

Sicily Campaign

For Operation Husky, the invasion of Sicily, Patton was to command the Seventh United States Army, dubbed the Western Task Force, in landings at Gela, Scoglitti and Licata to support landings by Bernard Montgomery's British Eighth Army. Patton's I Armored Corps was officially redesignated the Seventh Army just before his force of 90,000 landed before dawn on D-Day, July 10, 1943, on beaches near the town of Licata. The armada was hampered by wind and weather, but despite this the three U.S. infantry divisions involved, the 3rd, 1st, and 45th, secured their respective beaches. They then repulsed

Figure 8: *Patton near Brolo, Sicily, in 1943*

counterattacks at Gela,[105] where Patton personally led his troops against German reinforcements from the Hermann Göring Division.[106]

Initially ordered to protect the British forces' left flank, Patton was granted permission by Alexander to take Palermo after Montgomery's forces became bogged down on the road to Messina. As part of a provisional corps under Major General Geoffrey Keyes, the 3rd Infantry Division under Major General Lucian Truscott covered 100 miles (160 km) in 72 hours, arriving at Palermo on July 21. He then set his sights on Messina.[107] He sought an amphibious assault, but it was delayed by lack of landing craft, and his troops did not land at Santo Stefano until August 8, by which time the Germans and Italians had already evacuated the bulk of their troops to mainland Italy. He ordered more landings on August 10 by the 3rd Infantry Division, which took heavy casualties but pushed the German forces back, and hastened the advance on Messina.[108] A third landing was completed on August 16, and by 22:00 that day Messina fell to his forces. By the end of the battle, the 200,000-man Seventh Army had suffered 7,500 casualties, and killed or captured 113,000 Axis troops and destroyed 3,500 vehicles. Still, 40,000 German and 70,000 Italian troops escaped to Italy with 10,000 vehicles.[109,110]

Patton's conduct in this campaign met with several controversies. When Alexander sent a transmission on July 19 limiting Patton's attack on Messina,

Figure 9: *Patton talks to wounded soldiers preparing for evacuation*

his chief of staff, Brigadier General Hobart R. Gay, claimed the message was "lost in transmission" until Messina had fallen. On July 22 he shot and killed a pair of mules that had stopped while pulling a cart across a bridge. The cart was blocking the way of a U.S. armored column which was under attack from German aircraft. When their Sicilian owner protested, Patton attacked him with a walking stick and pushed the two mules off of the bridge.[107] When informed of the massacre of Italian prisoners at Biscari by troops under his command, Patton wrote in his diary, "I told Bradley that it was probably an exaggeration, but in any case to tell the officer to certify that the dead men were snipers or had attempted to escape or something, as it would make a stink in the press and also would make the civilians mad. Anyhow, they are dead, so nothing can be done about it."[111] Bradley refused Patton's suggestions. Patton later changed his mind. After he learned that the 45th Division's Inspector General found "no provocation on the part of the prisoners ... They had been slaughtered" Patton is reported to have said: "Try the bastards."[111] Patton also came into frequent disagreements with Terry de la Mesa Allen Sr. and Theodore Roosevelt Jr. and acquiesced to their relief by Bradley.[112]

Slapping incidents and aftermath

Two high-profile incidents of Patton striking subordinates during the Sicily campaign attracted national controversy following the end of the campaign.

On August 3, 1943, Patton slapped and verbally abused Private Charles H. Kuhl at an evacuation hospital in Nicosia after he had been found to suffer from "battle fatigue".[113] On August 10, Patton slapped Private Paul G. Bennett under similar circumstances.[113] Ordering both soldiers back to the front lines,[114] Patton railed against cowardice and issued orders to his commanders to discipline any soldier making similar complaints.[115]

Word of the incident reached Eisenhower, who privately reprimanded Patton and insisted he apologize.[116] Patton apologized to both soldiers individually, as well as to doctors who witnessed the incidents,[117] and later to all of the soldiers under his command in several speeches.[118] Eisenhower suppressed the incident in the media,[119] but in November journalist Drew Pearson revealed it on his radio program.[120] Criticism of Patton in the United States was harsh, and included members of Congress and former generals, Pershing among them.[121,122] The views of the general public remained mixed on the matter,[123] and eventually Secretary of War Henry L. Stimson stated that Patton must be retained as a commander because of the need for his "aggressive, winning leadership in the bitter battles which are to come before final victory."[124]

Patton did not command a force in combat for 11 months.[125] In September, Bradley, who was Patton's junior in both rank and experience, was selected to command the First United States Army forming in England to prepare for Operation Overlord.[126] This decision had been made before the slapping incidents were made public, but Patton blamed them for his being denied the command.[127] Eisenhower felt the invasion of Europe was too important to risk any uncertainty, and that the slapping incidents had been an example of Patton's inability to exercise discipline and self-control. While Eisenhower and Marshall both considered Patton to be a skilled combat commander, they felt Bradley was less impulsive or prone to making mistakes.[128] On January 26, 1944, Patton was formally given command of the U.S. Third Army in England, a newly formed field Army, and he was assigned to prepare its inexperienced soldiers for combat in Europe.[129,130] This duty kept Patton busy during the first half of 1944.[131]

Phantom Army

The German High Command had more respect for Patton than for any other Allied commander and considered him to be central to any plan to invade Europe from England.[132] Because of this, Patton was made a prominent figure in the deception operation, Fortitude, during the first half of 1944.[133] Through the British network of double-agents, the Allies fed German intelligence a steady stream of false reports about troops sightings and that Patton had been

named commander of the First United States Army Group (FUSAG), all designed to convince the Germans that Patton was preparing this massive command for an invasion at Pas de Calais. FUSAG was in reality an intricately
constructed fictitious army of decoys, props, and fake radio signal traffic based
around Dover to mislead German reconnaissance planes and to make Axis
leaders believe that a large force was massing there. This helped to mask the
real location of the invasion in Normandy. Patton was ordered to keep a low
profile to deceive the Germans into thinking that he was in Dover throughout
early 1944, when he was actually training the Third Army.[132] As a result of
Operation Fortitude, the German 15th Army remained at the Pas de Calais to
defend against Patton's supposed attack.[134] This German field army held its
position even after the invasion of Normandy on June 6, 1944. Patton flew to
France a month later, and then returned to combat command.[135]

Normandy breakout offensive

Sailing to Normandy throughout July, Patton's Third Army formed on the
extreme right (west) of the Allied land forces,[135,136]</ref> and became operational at noon on August 1, 1944, under Bradley's Twelfth United States
Army Group. The Third Army simultaneously attacked west into Brittany,
south, east toward the Seine, and north, assisting in trapping several hundred
thousand German soldiers in the Falaise Pocket between Falaise and Argentan.[137,138]

Patton's strategy with his army favored speed and aggressive offensive action, though his forces saw less opposition than did the other three Allied field
armies in the initial weeks of its advance.[139] The Third Army typically em-
ployed forward scout units to determine enemy strength and positions. Self-
propelled artillery moved with the spearhead units and was sited well forward,
ready to engage protected German positions with indirect fire. Light aircraft
such as the Piper L-4 Cub served as artillery spotters and provided airborne
reconnaissance. Once located, the armored infantry would attack using tanks
as infantry support. Other armored units would then break through enemy
lines and exploit any subsequent breach, constantly pressuring withdrawing
German forces to prevent them from regrouping and reforming a cohesive de-
fensive line.[140] The U.S. armor advanced using reconnaissance by fire, and
the .50 caliber M2 Browning heavy machine gun proved effective in this role,
often flushing out and killing German panzerfaust teams waiting in ambush as
well as breaking up German infantry assaults against the armored infantry.[141]

The speed of the advance forced Patton's units to rely heavily on air reconnaissance and tactical air support.[140] The Third Army had by far more military
intelligence (G-2) officers at headquarters specifically designated to coordi-
nate air strikes than any other army.[142] Its attached close air support group

was XIX Tactical Air Command, commanded by Brigadier General Otto P. Weyland. Developed originally by General Elwood Quesada of IX Tactical Air Command for the First Army in Operation Cobra, the technique of "armored column cover", in which close air support was directed by an air traffic controller in one of the attacking tanks, was used extensively by the Third Army. Each column was protected by a standing patrol of three to four P-47 and P-51 fighter-bombers as a combat air patrol (CAP).[143]

In its advance from Avranches to Argentan, the Third Army traversed 60 miles (97 km) in just two weeks. Patton's force was supplemented by Ultra intelligence for which he was briefed daily by his G-2, Colonel Oscar W. Koch, who apprised him of German counterattacks, and where to concentrate his forces.[144] Equally important to the advance of Third Army columns in northern France was the rapid advance of the supply echelons. Third Army logistics were overseen by Colonel Walter J. Muller, Patton's G-4, who emphasized flexibility, improvisation, and adaptation for Third Army supply echelons so forward units could rapidly exploit a breakthrough. Patton's rapid drive to Lorraine demonstrated his keen appreciation for the technological advantages of the U.S. Army. The major U.S. and Allied advantages were in mobility and air superiority. The U.S. Army had more trucks, more reliable tanks, and better radio communications, all of which contributed to a superior ability to operate at a rapid offensive pace.[145]

Lorraine Campaign

Patton's offensive came to a halt on August 31, 1944, as the Third Army ran out of fuel near the Moselle River, just outside Metz. Patton expected that the theater commander would keep fuel and supplies flowing to support successful advances, but Eisenhower favored a "broad front" approach to the ground-war effort, believing that a single thrust would have to drop off flank protection, and would quickly lose its punch. Still within the constraints of a very large effort overall, Eisenhower gave Montgomery and his Twenty First Army Group a higher priority for supplies for Operation Market Garden.[146] Combined with other demands on the limited resource pool, this resulted in the Third Army exhausting its fuel supplies.[147] Patton believed his forces were close enough to the Siegfried Line that he remarked to Bradley that with 400,000 gallons of gasoline he could be in Germany within two days.[148] In late September, a large German Panzer counterattack sent expressly to stop the advance of Patton's Third Army was defeated by the U.S. 4th Armored Division at the Battle of Arracourt. Despite the victory, the Third Army stayed in place as a result of Eisenhower's order. The German commanders believed this was because their counterattack had been successful.[149]

Figure 10: *Patton pins a Silver Star Medal on Private Ernest A. Jenkins, a soldier under his command, October 1944*

> 📺 *Booknotes* interview with Carlo D'Este on *Patton: A Genius for War*, January 28, 1996[150], C-SPAN

The halt of the Third Army during the month of September was enough to allow the Germans to strengthen the fortress of Metz. In October and November, the Third Army was mired in a near-stalemate with the Germans during the Battle of Metz, both sides suffering heavy casualties. An attempt by Patton to seize Fort Driant just south of Metz was defeated, but by mid-November Metz had fallen to the Americans.[151] Patton's decisions in taking this city were criticized. German commanders interviewed after the war noted he could have bypassed the city and moved north to Luxembourg where he would have been able to cut off the German Seventh Army.[152] The German commander of Metz, General Hermann Balck, also noted that a more direct attack would have resulted in a more decisive Allied victory in the city. Historian Carlo D'Este later wrote that the Lorraine Campaign was one of Patton's least successful, faulting him for not deploying his divisions more aggressively and decisively.[153]

Figure 11: *Bradley, Eisenhower and Patton (right) in Bastogne, Belgium, 1945*

With supplies low and priority given to Montgomery until the port of Antwerp could be opened, Patton remained frustrated at the lack of progress of his forces. From November 8 to December 15, his army advanced no more than 40 miles (64 km).[154]

Battle of the Bulge

In December 1944, the German army, under the command of German Field Marshal Gerd von Rundstedt, launched a last-ditch offensive across Belgium, Luxembourg, and northeastern France. On December 16, 1944, it massed 29 divisions totaling 250,000 men at a weak point in the Allied lines, and during the early stages of the ensuing Battle of the Bulge, made significant headway towards the Meuse River during the worst winter Europe had seen in years. Eisenhower called a meeting of all senior Allied commanders on the Western Front to a headquarters near Verdun on the morning of December 19 to plan strategy and a response to the German assault.[155]

At the time, Patton's Third Army was engaged in heavy fighting near Saar-brücken. Guessing the intent of the Allied command meeting, Patton ordered his staff to make three separate operational contingency orders to disengage elements of the Third Army from its present position and begin offensive operations toward several objectives in the area of the bulge occupied by German forces.[156] At the Supreme Command conference, Eisenhower led the meeting, which was attended by Patton, Bradley, General Jacob Devers, Major General Kenneth Strong, Deputy Supreme Commander Air Chief Marshal Arthur Tedder, and several staff officers.[157] When Eisenhower asked Patton how long it would take him to disengage six divisions of his Third Army and commence a counterattack north to relieve the U.S. 101st Airborne Division which had been trapped at Bastogne, Patton replied, "As soon as you're through with me."[158] Patton then clarified that he had already worked up an operational order for a counterattack by three full divisions on December 21, then only 48 hours away.[158] Eisenhower was incredulous: "Don't be fatuous, George. If you try to go that early you won't have all three divisions ready and you'll go piecemeal." Patton replied that his staff already had a contingency operations order ready to go. Still unconvinced, Eisenhower ordered Patton to attack the morning of December 22, using at least three divisions.[159]

Patton left the conference room, phoned his command, and uttered two words: "Play ball." This code phrase initiated a prearranged operational order with Patton's staff, mobilizing three divisions – the 4th Armored Division, the U.S. 80th Infantry Division, and the U.S. 26th Infantry Division – from the Third Army and moving them north toward Bastogne.[156] In all, Patton would reposition six full divisions, U.S. III Corps and U.S. XII Corps, from their positions on the Saar River front along a line stretching from Bastogne to Diekirch and to Echternach, the town in Luxembourg that had been at the southern end of the initial "Bulge" front line on December 16.[160] Within a few days, more than 133,000 Third Army vehicles were rerouted into an offensive that covered an average distance of over 11 miles (18 km) per vehicle, followed by support echelons carrying 62,000 tonnes (61,000 long tons; 68,000 short tons) of supplies.[161]

On December 21, Patton met with Bradley to review the impending advance, starting the meeting by remarking, "Brad, this time the Kraut's stuck his head in the meat grinder, and I've got hold of the handle."[156] Patton then argued that his Third Army should attack toward Koblenz, cutting off the bulge at the base and trap the entirety of the German armies involved in the offensive. After briefly considering this, Bradley vetoed it, since he was less concerned about killing large numbers of Germans than he was in arranging for the relief of Bastogne before it was overrun.[159] Desiring good weather for his advance, which would permit close ground support by U.S. Army Air Forces tactical aircraft, Patton ordered the Third Army chaplain, Colonel James Hugh O'Neill, to compose a suitable prayer. He responded with: <templatestyles src="Template:Quote/styles.css"/>

Almighty and most merciful Father, we humbly beseech Thee, of Thy great goodness, to restrain these immoderate rains with which we have had to

contend. Grant us fair weather for Battle. Graciously hearken to us as
soldiers who call upon Thee that, armed with Thy power, we may advance
from victory to victory and crush the oppression and wickedness of our
enemies, and establish Thy justice among men and nations. Amen.[119]

When the weather cleared soon after, Patton awarded O'Neill a Bronze Star
Medal on the spot.[119]

On December 26, 1944, the first spearhead units of the Third Army's 4th
Armored Division reached Bastogne, opening a corridor for relief and resupply
of the besieged forces. Patton's ability to disengage six divisions from front line
combat during the middle of winter, then wheel north to relieve Bastogne was
one of his most remarkable achievements during the war.[162] He later wrote
that the relief of Bastogne was "the most brilliant operation we have thus far
performed, and it is in my opinion the outstanding achievement of the war.
This is my biggest battle."[161]

Advance into Germany

By February, the Germans were in full retreat. On February 23, 1945, the U.S.
94th Infantry Division crossed the Saar River and established a vital bridgehead
at Serrig, through which Patton pushed units into the Saarland. Patton had
insisted upon an immediate crossing of the Saar River against the advice of
his officers. Historians such as Charles Whiting have criticized this strategy as
unnecessarily aggressive.[163]

Once again, Patton found other commands given priority on gasoline and supplies.[164] To obtain these, Third Army ordnance units passed themselves off as
First Army personnel and in one incident they secured thousands of gallons
of gasoline from a First Army dump.[165] Between January 29 and March 22,
the Third Army took Trier, Coblenz, Bingen, Worms, Mainz, Kaiserslautern,
and Ludwigshafen, killing or wounding 99,000 and capturing 140,112 German soldiers, which represented virtually all of the remnants of the German
First and Seventh Armies. An example of Patton's sarcastic wit was broadcast when he received orders to bypass Trier, as it had been decided that four
divisions would be needed to capture it. When the message arrived, Trier had
already fallen. Patton rather caustically replied: "Have taken Trier with two
divisions. Do you want me to give it back?"[166]

The Third Army began crossing the Rhine River after constructing a pontoon
bridge on March 22, and he slipped a division across the river that evening.[167]
Patton later boasted he had urinated into the river as he crossed.[168]

On March 26, 1945, Patton sent Task Force Baum, consisting of 314 men, 16
tanks, and assorted other vehicles, 50 miles (80 km) behind German lines to
liberate the prisoner of war camp OFLAG XIII-B, near Hammelburg. Patton

Figure 12: *Eisenhower, Bradley and Patton inspect a cremation pyre at the Ohrdruf concentration camp on April 12, 1945, after liberation.*

knew that one of the inmates was his son-in-law, Lieutenant Colonel John K. Waters. The raid was a failure, and only 35 men made it back; the rest were either killed or captured, and all 57 vehicles were lost. Another prisoner liberated from the Oflag was Lt. Donald Prell who was recaptured and was sent to a POW camp south of Nuremberg. Patton reported this attempt to liberate Oflag XIII-B as the only mistake he made during World War II.[169] When Eisenhower learned of the secret mission, he was furious.[170] Patton later said he felt the correct decision would have been to send a Combat Command, which is a force about three times larger.[169]

By April, resistance against the Third Army was tapering off, and the forces' main efforts turned to managing some 400,000 German prisoners of war.[170] On April 14, 1945, Patton was promoted to general, a promotion long advocated by Stimson in recognition of Patton's battle accomplishments during 1944.[171] Later that month, Patton, Bradley, and Eisenhower toured the Merkers salt mine as well as the Ohrdruf concentration camp, and seeing the conditions of the camp firsthand caused Patton great disgust. Third Army was ordered toward Bavaria and Czechoslovakia, anticipating a last stand by Nazi German forces there. He was reportedly appalled to learn that the Red Army would take Berlin, feeling that the Soviet Union was a threat to the U.S. Army's advance to Pilsen, but was stopped by Eisenhower from reaching

Figure 13: *Patton during a welcome home parade in Los Angeles, June 9, 1945*

Prague, Czechoslovakia, before V-E Day on May 8 and the end of the war in Europe.[172]

In its advance from the Rhine to the Elbe, Patton's Third Army, which numbered between 250,000 and 300,000 men at any given time, captured 32,763 square miles (84,860 km^2) of German territory. Its losses were 2,102 killed, 7,954 wounded, and 1,591 missing. German losses in the fighting against the Third Army totaled 20,100 killed, 47,700 wounded, and 653,140 captured.[173]

Between becoming operational in Normandy on August 1, 1944, and the end of hostilities on May 9, 1945, the Third Army was in continuous combat for 281 days. In that time, it crossed 24 major rivers and captured 81,500 square miles (211,000 km^2) of territory, including more than 12,000 cities and towns. The Third Army claimed to have killed, wounded, or captured 1,811,388 German soldiers, six times its strength in personnel.[173] Fuller's review of Third Army records differs only in the number of enemy killed and wounded, stating that between August 1, 1944, and May 9, 1945, 47,500 of the enemy were killed, 115,700 wounded, and 1,280,688 captured, for a total of 1,443,888.[174]

Postwar

Patton asked for a command in the Pacific Theater of Operations, begging Marshall to bring him to that war in any way possible, and Marshall said he would be able to do so only if the Chinese secured a major port for his entry, an unlikely scenario.[172] In mid-May, Patton flew to Paris, then London for rest. On June 7, he arrived in Bedford, Massachusetts, for extended leave with his family, and was greeted by thousands of spectators. Patton then drove to Hatch Memorial Shell and spoke to some 20,000, including a crowd of 400 wounded Third Army veterans. In this speech he aroused some controversy among the Gold Star Mothers when he stated that a man who dies in battle is "frequently a fool",[175] adding that the wounded are heroes. Patton spent time in Boston before visiting and speaking in Denver and visiting Los Angeles, where he spoke to a crowd of 100,000 at the Memorial Coliseum. Patton made a final stop in Washington, D.C. before returning to Europe in July to serve in the occupation forces.[176]

On 14 June 1945, Secretary of War Henry L. Stimson announced that Patton would not be sent to the Pacific but would return to Europe in an occupation army assignment.[177]

Patton was appointed as then military governor of Bavaria, where he led the Third Army in denazification efforts.[176] Patton was particularly upset when learning of the end of the war against Japan, writing in his diary, "Yet another war has come to an end, and with it my usefulness to the world."[176] Unhappy with his position and depressed by his belief that he would never fight in another war, Patton's behavior and statements became increasingly erratic. Various explanations beyond his disappointments have been proposed for Patton's behavior at this point. Carlo D'Este wrote that "it seems virtually inevitable ... that Patton experienced some type of brain damage from too many head injuries" from a lifetime of numerous auto- and horse-related accidents, especially one suffered while playing polo in 1936.[119]

Patton's niece Jean Gordon appeared again; they spent some time together in London in 1944, and again in Bavaria in 1945. Gordon actually loved a young married captain who left her despondent when he went home to his wife in September 1945.[178] Patton repeatedly boasted of his sexual success with Gordon, but his biographers are skeptical. Hirshson said that the relationship was casual.[179] Showalter believes that Patton, under severe physical and psychological stress, made up claims of sexual conquest to prove his virility.[180] D'Este agrees, saying, "His behavior suggests that in both 1936 [in Hawaii] and 1944–45, the presence of the young and attractive Jean was a means of assuaging the anxieties of a middle-aged man troubled over his virility and a fear of aging."[181]

Patton attracted controversy as military governor when it was noted that several former Nazi Party members continued to hold political posts in the region.[176] When responding to the press about the subject, Patton repeatedly compared Nazis to Democrats and Republicans in noting that most of the people with

Figure 14: *Patton's grave in Luxembourg City*

experience in infrastructure management had been compelled to join the party in the war, causing negative press stateside and angering Eisenhower.[182,183] On September 28, 1945, after a heated exchange with Eisenhower over his statements, Patton was relieved of his military governorship. He was relieved of command of the Third Army on October 7, and in a somber change of command ceremony, Patton concluded his farewell remarks, "All good things must come to an end. The best thing that has ever happened to me thus far is the honor and privilege of having commanded the Third Army."[182]

Patton's final assignment was to command the U.S. 15th Army, based in Bad Nauheim. The 15th Army at this point consisted only of a small headquarters staff working to compile a history of the war in Europe. Patton had accepted the post because of his love of history, but quickly lost interest. He began traveling, visiting Paris, Rennes, Chartres, Brussels, Metz, Reims, Luxembourg, and Verdun. Then he went to[182] Stockholm, where he reunited with other athletes from the 1912 Olympics. Patton decided that he would leave his post at the 15th Army and not return to Europe once he left on December 10 for Christmas leave. He intended to discuss with his wife whether he would continue in a stateside post or retire from the Army.[184]

Accident and death

On December 8, 1945, Patton's chief of staff, Major General Hobart Gay, invited him on a pheasant hunting trip near Speyer to lift his spirits. Observing derelict cars along the side of the road, Patton said, "How awful war is. Think of the waste." Moments later his car collided with an American army truck at low speed.[184,185]

Gay and others were only slightly injured, but Patton hit his head on the glass partition in the back seat. He began bleeding from a gash to the head, and complained that he was paralyzed and having trouble breathing. Taken to a hospital in Heidelberg, Patton was discovered to have a compression fracture and dislocation of the cervical third and fourth vertebrae, resulting in a broken neck and cervical spinal cord injury that rendered him paralyzed from the neck down.[185]

Patton spent most of the next 12 days in spinal traction to decrease the pressure on his spine. All nonmedical visitors, except for Patton's wife, who had flown from the U.S., were forbidden. Patton, who had been told he had no chance to ever again ride a horse or resume normal life, at one point commented, "This is a hell of a way to die." He died in his sleep of pulmonary edema and congestive heart failure at about 18:00 on December 21, 1945.[186] Speculation as to whether the collision and Patton's injuries and death resulted from mere accident or a deliberate assassination continued into the twenty-first century.[187]

Patton was buried at the Luxembourg American Cemetery and Memorial in the Hamm district of Luxembourg City, alongside some wartime casualties of the Third Army, in accordance with his request to "be buried with [his] men".

Legacy

Patton's colorful personality, hard-driving leadership style, and success as a commander, combined with his frequent political missteps, produced a mixed and often contradictory image. Patton's great oratory skill is seen as integral to his ability to inspire troops under his command.[188] Historian Terry Brighton concluded that Patton was "arrogant, publicity-seeking and personally flawed, but ... among the greatest generals of the war".[189] Patton's impact on armored warfare and leadership were substantial, with the U.S. Army's adopting many of Patton's aggressive strategies for its training programs following his death. Many military officers claim inspiration from his legacy. The first American tank designed after the war became the M46 Patton.[190]

Several actors have portrayed Patton on screen, the most famous being George C. Scott in the 1970 film *Patton*. Scott's iconic depiction of Patton earned him

Figure 15: *General Patton U.S. commemorative stamp, issued in 1953*

an Academy Award for Best Actor, and it was instrumental in bringing Patton into popular culture as a folk hero.[191] He would reprise the role in 1986 in the made-for-television film *The Last Days of Patton*. Other actors who have portrayed Patton include Stephen McNally in the 1957 episode "The Patton Prayer" of the ABC religion anthology series, *Crossroads*, John Larch in the 1963 film *Miracle of the White Stallions*, Kirk Douglas in the 1966 film *Is Paris Burning?*, George Kennedy in the 1978 film *Brass Target*, Darren McGavin in the 1979 miniseries *Ike*, Robert Prentiss in the 1988 film *Pancho Barnes*, Mitchell Ryan in the 1989 film *Double Exposure: The Story of Margaret Bourke-White*, Lawrence Dobkin in a 1989 episode of the miniseries *War and Remembrance*, Edward Asner in the 1997 film *The Long Way Home*, Gerald McRaney in the 2004 miniseries *Ike: Countdown to D-Day*, Dan Higgins in a 2006 episode of the miniseries *Man, Moment, Machine*, and Kelsey Grammer in the 2008 film *An American Carol*.

Image

Patton deliberately cultivated a flashy, distinctive image in the belief that this would inspire his troops. He carried an ivory-gripped, engraved, silver-plated Colt Single Action Army .45 caliber revolver on his right hip, and frequently wore an ivory-gripped Smith & Wesson Model 27 .357 Magnum on his left hip.[39,192] He was usually seen wearing a highly polished helmet, riding pants, and high cavalry boots.[193] Likewise, Patton cultivated a stern expression he called his "war face".[92] He was known to oversee training maneuvers from

Figure 16: *A replica of Patton's World War II command vehicle on display at the Lone Star Flight Museum in Houston, Texas.*

atop a tank painted red, white and blue. His jeep bore oversized rank placards on the front and back, as well as a klaxon horn which would loudly announce his approach from afar. He proposed a new uniform for the emerging Tank Corps, featuring polished buttons, a gold helmet, and thick, dark padded suits; the proposal was derided in the media as "the Green Hornet", and it was rejected by the Army.[85]

The historian Alan Axelrod wrote that "for Patton, leadership was never simply about making plans and giving orders, it was about transforming oneself into a symbol".[88] Patton intentionally expressed a conspicuous desire for glory, atypical of the officer corps of the day which emphasized blending in with troops on the battlefield. He was an admirer of Admiral Horatio Nelson for his actions in leading the Battle of Trafalgar in a full dress uniform.[88] Patton had a preoccupation with bravery,[7] wearing his rank insignia conspicuously in combat, and at one point during World War II, he rode atop a tank into a German-controlled village seeking to inspire courage in his men.[62]

Patton was a staunch fatalist,[194] and he believed in reincarnation. He believed that he might have been a military leader killed in action in Napoleon's army in a previous life, or a Roman legionary.[3,195]

Patton developed an ability to deliver charismatic speeches.[75] He used profanity heavily in his speech, which generally was enjoyed by troops under his command, but it offended other generals, including Bradley.[196] The most famous of his speeches were a series he delivered to the Third Army prior to Operation Overlord.[197] When speaking, he was known for his bluntness and witticism; he once said, "The two most dangerous weapons the Germans have are our own armored halftrack and jeep. The halftrack because the boys in it go all heroic, thinking they are in a tank. The jeep because we have so many God-awful drivers. "[198] During the Battle of the Bulge, he famously remarked that the Allies should "let the sons-of-bitches [Germans] go all the way to Paris, then we'll cut them off and round them up."[198] He also suggested facetiously that his Third Army could "drive the British back into the sea for another Dunkirk."[198]

As media scrutiny on Patton increased, his bluntness stirred controversy. These began in North Africa when some reporters worried that he was becoming too close to former Vichy officials with Axis sympathies.[199] His public image was more seriously damaged after word of the slapping incidents broke.[200] Another controversy occurred prior to Operation Overlord when Patton spoke at a British welcoming club at Knutsford in England, and said, in part, "since it is the evident destiny of the British and Americans, and of course, the Russians, to rule the world, the better we know each other, the better job we will do." The next day news accounts misquoted Patton by leaving off the Russians.[201]

On a visit home after the war he again made headlines when he attempted to honor several wounded veterans in a speech by calling them "the real heroes" of the war, unintentionally offending the families of soldiers who had been killed in action.[176] His final media blowup occurred in September 1945, when goaded by reporters about denazification, he said "[d]enazification would be like removing all the Republicans and all the Democrats who were in office, who had held office or were quasi-Democrats or Republicans and that would take some time." This caused Eisenhower to relieve Patton from command of the Third Army.[202]

As a leader, Patton was known to be highly critical, correcting subordinates mercilessly for the slightest infractions, but also being quick to praise their accomplishments.[85] Although he garnered a reputation as a general who was both impatient and impulsive and had little tolerance for officers who had failed to succeed, he fired only one general during World War II, Orlando Ward, and only after two warnings, whereas Bradley sacked several generals during the war.[203] Patton reportedly had the utmost respect for the men serving in his command, particularly the wounded.[204] Many of his directives showed special trouble to care for the enlisted men under his command, and he was well known

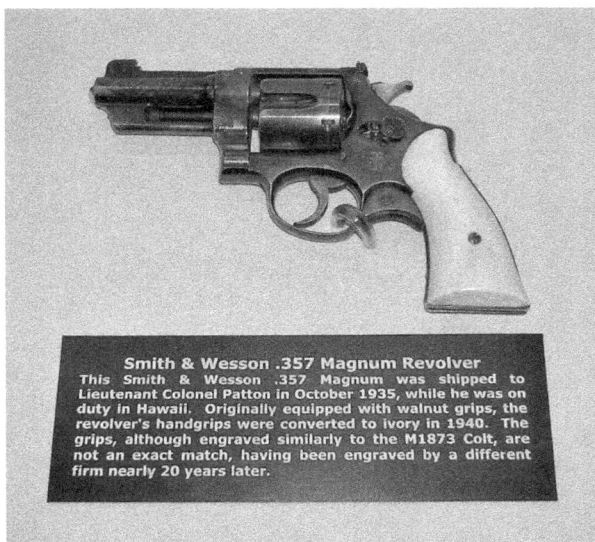

Smith & Wesson .357 Magnum Revolver
This Smith & Wesson .357 Magnum was shipped to Lieutenant Colonel Patton in October 1935, while he was on duty in Hawaii. Originally equipped with walnut grips, the revolver's handgrips were converted to ivory in 1940. The grips, although engraved similarly to the M1873 Colt, are not an exact match, having been engraved by a different firm nearly 20 years later.

Figure 17: *Patton's well-known custom ivory-handled revolver*

for arranging extra supplies for battlefield soldiers, including blankets and extra socks, galoshes, and other items normally in short supply at the front.[205]

Patton's views on race were complicated and often negative. This may have resulted from his privileged upbringing and family roots in the southern United States.[206] Privately he wrote of black soldiers: "Individually they were good soldiers, but I expressed my belief at the time, and have never found the necessity of changing it, that a colored soldier cannot think fast enough to fight in armor."[207] He also stated that performance was more important than race or religious affiliation: "I don't give a damn who the man is. He can be a Nigger or a Jew, but if he has the stuff and does his duty, he can have anything I've got. By God! I love him."[208]

Addressing the 761st Tank Battalion Patton also said, "Men, you are the first Negro tankers ever to fight in the American Army. I would never have asked for you if you weren't good. I have nothing but the best in my army. I don't care what color you are, so long as you go up there and kill those Kraut sonsabitches! Everyone has their eyes on you and is expecting great things from you. Most of all, your race is looking forward to you. Don't let them down and, damn you, don't let me down!"[209] Likewise, Patton called heavily on the Black troops under his command.[194] Historian Hugh Cole notes that Patton was the first to integrate black and white soldiers into the same rifle companies.[209]

Figure 18: *A statue of Patton at the US Military Academy at West Point*

After reading the Koran and observing North Africans, he wrote to his wife, "Just finished reading the Koran – a good book and interesting." Patton had a keen eye for native customs and methods and wrote knowingly of local architecture; he once rated the progress of word-of-mouth rumor in Arab country at 40–60 miles (64–97 km) a day. In spite of his regard for the Koran, he concluded, "To me it seems certain that the fatalistic teachings of Mohammad and the utter degradation of women is the outstanding cause for the arrested development of the Arab ... Here, I think, is a text for some eloquent sermon on the virtues of Christianity."[210]

Patton was impressed with the Soviet Union but was disdainful of Russians as "drunks" with "no regard for human life".[211] Later in life he also began to express growing feelings of antisemitism and anticommunism, as a result of his frequent controversies in the press.[182]

As viewed by Allied and Axis leaders

On February 1, 1945, Eisenhower wrote a memo ranking the military capabilities of his subordinate American generals in Europe. General Bradley and the Army Air Forces General Carl Spaatz shared the number one position, Walter Bedell Smith was ranked number two, and Patton number three.[212] Eisenhower revealed his reasoning in a 1946 review of the book *Patton and His*

Third Army: "George Patton was the most brilliant commander of an Army in the open field that our or any other service produced. But his army was part of a whole organization and his operations part of a great campaign."[213] Eisenhower believed that other generals such as Bradley should be given the credit for planning the successful Allied campaigns across Europe in which Patton was merely "a brilliant executor".[213]

Notwithstanding Eisenhower's estimation of Patton's abilities as a strategic planner, his overall view of Patton's military value in achieving Allied victory in Europe is revealed in his refusal to even consider sending Patton home after the slapping incidents of 1943, after which he privately remarked, "Patton is indispensable to the war effort – one of the guarantors of our victory."[214] As Assistant Secretary of War John J. McCloy told Eisenhower: "Lincoln's remark after they got after Grant comes to mind when I think of Patton – 'I can't spare this man, he fights'."[215] After Patton's death, Eisenhower would write his own tribute: "He was one of those men born to be a soldier, an ideal combat leader ... It is no exaggeration to say that Patton's name struck terror at the hearts of the enemy."[213]

Carlo D'Este insisted that Bradley disliked Patton both personally and professionally,[216,217] but Bradley's biographer Jim DeFelice noted that the evidence indicates otherwise.[218] President Franklin D. Roosevelt appeared to greatly esteem Patton and his abilities, stating "he is our greatest fighting general, and sheer joy".[219] On the other hand, Roosevelt's successor, Harry S. Truman, appears to have taken an instant dislike to Patton, at one point comparing both him and Douglas MacArthur to George Armstrong Custer.[219]

For the most part, British commanders did not hold Patton in high regard. General Sir Alan Brooke, the Chief of the Imperial General Staff (CIGS) – the professional head of the British Army – noted in January 1943 that "I had heard of him, but I must confess that his swashbuckling personality exceeded my expectation. I did not form any high opinion of him, nor had I any reason to alter this view at any later date. A dashing, courageous, wild, and unbalanced leader, good for operations requiring thrust and push, but at a loss in any operation requiring skill and judgment."[220]

One possible exception was Field Marshal Sir Bernard Montgomery who appears to have admired Patton's ability to command troops in the field, if not his strategic judgment.[221] Other Allied commanders were more impressed, the Free French in particular. General Henri Giraud was incredulous when he heard of Patton's dismissal by Eisenhower in late 1945, and invited him to Paris to be decorated by President Charles de Gaulle at a state banquet. At the banquet, President de Gaulle gave a speech placing Patton's achievements alongside those of Napoleon.[222] Soviet leader Joseph Stalin was apparently an

Figure 19: *Patton's boots at a museum in Malmedy*

admirer, stating that the Red Army could neither have planned nor executed Patton's rapid armored advance across France.[223]

While Allied leaders expressed mixed feelings on Patton's capabilities, the German High Command was noted to have more respect for him than for any other Allied commander after 1943.[132] Adolf Hitler reportedly called him "that crazy cowboy general".[224] Many German field commanders were generous in their praise of Patton's leadership following the war,[225] *General der Panzertruppen* Hasso von Manteuffel, who had fought both Soviet and Anglo-American tank commanders, agreed: "Patton! No doubt about this. He was a brilliant Panzer army commander."[160]</ref> and many of its highest commanders also held his abilities in high regard. Erwin Rommel credited Patton with executing "the most astonishing achievement in mobile warfare".[226] *Generaloberst* Alfred Jodl, chief of staff of the German Army, stated that Patton "was the American Guderian. He was very bold and preferred large movements. He took big risks and won big successes."[224] *Generalfeldmarschall* Albert Kesselring noted that "Patton had developed tank warfare into an art, and understood how to handle tanks brilliantly in the field. I feel compelled, therefore, to compare him with *Generalfeldmarschall* Rommel, who likewise had mastered the art of tank warfare. Both of them had a kind of second sight in regard to this type of warfare."[224] Referring to the escape of the Afrika Korps after the Battle of El Alamein, Fritz Bayerlein opined that "I do not think that General Patton would let us get away so easily."[224] In an interview conducted for *Stars and Stripes* just after his capture, Field Marshal Gerd von Rundstedt stated simply of Patton, "He is your best."[227]

Notes

References

<templatestyles src="Template:Refbegin/styles.css" />

- Allen, Thomas; Dickson, Paul (2006), *The Bonus Army: An American Epic*, London: Walker & Company, ISBN 978-0-8027-7738-6
- Ambrose, Stephen E. (2007), *Eisenhower: Soldier and President*, New York City: Simon & Schuster, ISBN 978-0-945707-39-4
- Atkinson, Rick (2007), *The Day of Battle: The War in Sicily and Italy, 1943–1944 (The Liberation Trilogy)*, New York City: Henry Holt and Company, ISBN 0-8050-6289-0
- Axelrod, Alan (2006), *Patton: A Biography*, London: Palgrave Macmillan, ISBN 978-1-4039-7139-5
- Blumenson, Martin (1972), *The Patton Papers: 1885–1940*, Boston, Massachusetts: Houghton Mifflin, ISBN 0-395-12706-8
- Blumenson, Martin (1974), *The Patton Papers: 1940–1945*, Boston: Houghton Mifflin, ISBN 0-395-18498-3
- Blumenson, Martin (1985), *Patton: The Man Behind the Legend*, New York City: William Morrow and Company, ISBN 978-0-688-13795-3
- Brighton, Terry (2009), *Patton, Montgomery, Rommel: Masters of War*, New York City: Crown Publishing Group, ISBN 978-0-307-46154-4
- DeFelice, Jim (2011), *Omar Bradley: General at War*, Washington, DC: Regenery History, ISBN 978-1-59698-139-3
- D'Este, Carlo (1995), *Patton: A Genius for War*, New York City: Harper Collins, ISBN 0-06-016455-7
- D'Este, Carlo (2002), *Eisenhower: A Soldier's Life*, New York City: Henry Holt and Company, ISBN 978-0-8050-5687-7
- Edey, Maitland A. (1968), *Time Capsule 1943*, London: Littlehampton Book Services, ISBN 978-0-7054-0270-5
- Essame, H. (1974), *Patton: A Study in Command*, New York City: Scribner & Sons, ISBN 978-0-684-13671-4
- Evans, Colin (2001), *Great feuds in history : ten of the liveliest disputes ever*, New York City: John Wiley and Sons, ISBN 0-471-38038-5
- Farago, Ladislas (1964), *Patton: Ordeal and Triumph*, New York City: Ivan Sergeyevich Obolensky, ISBN 1-59416-011-2
- Fuller, Robert P. (2004), *Last shots for Patton's Third Army*, Portland, Maine: NETR Press, ISBN 0-9740519-0-X
- Gooderson, Ian (1998), *Air Power at the Battlefront: Allied Close Air Support in Europe 1943–45*, Portland, Oregon: Routledge, ISBN 978-0-7146-4211-6

- Hirshson, Stanley (2003), *General Patton: A Soldier's Life*, New York City: Harper Perennial, ISBN 978-0-06-000983-0
- Hunt, David (1990) [1966], *A Don at War* (revised ed.), Great Britain: Frank Cass, ISBN 0-7146-3383-6
- Jarymowycz, Roman J. (2001), *Tank tactics: from Normandy to Lorraine*, Boulder, Colorado: Lynne Rienner Publishers, ISBN 1-55587-950-0
- Jowett, Philip; de Quesada, Alejandro (2006), *The Mexican Revolution 1910–20*, London: Osprey Publishing, p. 25, ISBN 978-1-84176-989-9
- Le Tissier, Tony (2007), *Patton's Pawns: The 94th US Infantry Division at the Siegfried Line*, Tuscaloosa, Alabama: University of Alabama Press, ISBN 0-8173-1557-8
- Lovelace, Alexander G. (2014), "The Image of a General: The Wartime Relationship between General George S. Patton Jr. and the American Media", *Journalism History*, **40** (no. 2 (Summer 2014)), pp. 108–120
- McNeese, Tim (2003), *Great Battles through the Ages: Battle of the Bulge*, New York City: Chelsea House Publications, ISBN 978-0-7910-7435-0
- Patton, George S. (1947), *War as I Knew It*, Boston, Massachusetts: Houghton Mifflin Co., ISBN 978-1-4193-2492-5
- Regan, Geoffrey (1992), *Military Anecdotes*, Enfield, Middlesex: Guinness Publishing, ISBN 0-85112-519-0
- Rice, Earl (2004), *George S. Patton*, Sagebrush Education Resources, ISBN 978-1-4176-2100-2
- Rickard, John Nelson (2004), *Patton at Bay: The Lorraine Campaign, September to December 1944*, Dulles, Virginia: Brassey's Inc., ISBN 1-57488-782-3
- Showalter, Dennis E. (2006), *Patton And Rommel: Men of War in the Twentieth Century* (2006 ed.), New York City: Berkley Books, ISBN 978-0-425-20663-8
- Steele, Brett D. (2005), *Military Reengineering Between the World Wars*, Chicago: Rand Publishing, ISBN 978-0-8330-3721-3
- von Mellenthin, Frederick W. (2006), *Panzer Battles: A Study of the Employment of Armor in the Second World War*, Old Saybrook, Connecticut: Konecky & Konecky, ISBN 978-1-56852-578-5
- Wallace, Brenton G. (1946), *Patton & His Third Army*, Harrisburg, Pennsylvania: Military Service Publishing Co., ISBN 0-8117-2896-X
- Zaloga, Steven (2008), *Armored Thunderbolt: The U.S. Army Sherman in World War II*, Mechanicsburg, Pennsylvania: Stackpole Books, ISBN 978-0-8117-0424-3
- Zaloga, Steven (2010), *George S. Patton: Leadership, Strategy, Conflict*[228], Oxford, United Kingdom: Osprey Publishing, ISBN 978-1-

84603-459-6

External links

- Cadet Patton at VMI[229] Virginia Military Institute Archives
- General George Patton Museum[230]
- Patton Uncovered[231] at the Wayback Machine (archived June 28, 2007)
- Lost Victory – Strasbourg, November 1944[232]
- National Museum of Military History[233]
- The General George S. Patton Story[234] on YouTube, United States Army, from *The Big Picture*, narrated by Ronald Reagan
- The short film *The General George S. Patton Story*[235] is available for free download at the Internet Archive
- George S. Patton Papers: Diaries, 1910-1945[236] at Library of Congress

Awards and achievements		
Preceded by **Sir Thomas Beecham Walter F. George Matthew Ridgway**	**Cover of Time Magazine** April 12, 1943 July 26, 1943 April 9, 1945	Succeeded by **Manuel Ávila Camacho Ingrid Bergman Simon Bolivar Buckner Jr.**
Military offices		
Preceded by **Charles L. Scott**	**Commanding General 2nd Armored Division** 1941–1942	Succeeded by **Willis D. Crittenberger**
Preceded by **Charles L. Scott**	**Commanding General I Armored Corps** 1942–1943	Succeeded by **Geoffrey Keyes**
Preceded by **Lloyd Fredendall**	**Commanding General II Corps** March 1943 – April 1943	Succeeded by **Omar Bradley**
Preceded by **Newly activated post**	**Commanding General Seventh Army** 1943–1944	Succeeded by **Mark W. Clark**
Preceded by **Courtney Hodges**	**Commanding General Third Army** 1944–1945	Succeeded by **Lucian Truscott**
Preceded by **Leonard T. Gerow**	**Commanding General Fifteenth Army** October 1945 – December 1945	Succeeded by **Hobart R. Gay**

<indicator name="featured-star"> ⭐ </indicator>

George S. Patton slapping incidents

George S. Patton slapping incidents

<indicator name="featured-star"> ⭐ </indicator>

In early August 1943, Lieutenant General George S. Patton slapped two United States Army soldiers under his command during the Sicily Campaign of World War II. Patton's hard-driving personality and lack of belief in the medical condition combat stress reaction, then known as "battle fatigue" or "shell shock", led to the soldiers becoming the subject of his ire in incidents on 3 and 10 August, when Patton struck and berated them after discovering they were patients at evacuation hospitals away from the front lines without apparent physical injuries.

Word of the incidents spread, eventually reaching Patton's superior, General Dwight D. Eisenhower, who ordered him to apologize to the men. Patton's actions were initially suppressed in the news until journalist Drew Pearson publicized them in the United States. While the U.S. Congress and the general public expressed both support and disdain for Patton's actions, Eisenhower and Army Chief of Staff George Marshall opted not to fire Patton as a commander. He was nonetheless sidelined from combat command for almost a year.

Seizing the opportunity the predicament presented, Eisenhower used Patton as a decoy in Operation Fortitude, sending faulty intelligence to German agents that Patton was leading the Invasion of Europe. While Patton eventually returned to combat command in the European Theater in mid-1944, the slapping incidents were seen by Eisenhower, Marshall, and other leaders to be examples of Patton's brashness and impulsiveness. Patton's career was halted as former subordinates such as Omar Bradley became his superiors.

Figure 20: *Lieutenant General George S. Patton, com-*
mander of the Seventh United States Army, in 1943

Background

The Allied invasion of Sicily began on 10 July 1943, with Lieutenant General
George S. Patton landing 90,000 men of the Seventh United States Army near
Gela, Scoglitti, and Licata to support Bernard Montgomery's British 8th Army
landings to the north.[237] Initially ordered to protect the British forces' flank,
Patton took Palermo after Montgomery's forces were slowed by heavy resistance from troops of Nazi Germany and the Kingdom of Italy. Patton then set
his sights on Messina.[238] He sought an amphibious assault, but it was delayed
by lack of landing craft and his troops did not land in Santo Stefano until 8 August, by which time the Germans and Italians had already evacuated the bulk
of their troops to mainland Italy. Throughout the campaign, Patton's troops
were heavily engaged by German and Italian forces as they pushed across the
island.[239]

Patton had already developed a reputation in the U.S. Army as an effective, successful, and hard-driving commander, punishing subordinates for the
slightest infractions but also rewarding them when they performed well.[240] As
a way to promote an image that inspired his troops, Patton created a larger-
than-life personality. He became known for his flashy dress, highly polished

helmet and boots, and no-nonsense demeanor.[241] General Dwight D. Eisenhower, the commander of the Sicily operation and Patton's friend and commanding officer, had long known of Patton's colorful leadership style, and also knew that Patton was prone to impulsiveness and a lack of self-restraint.[242]

Battle fatigue

Prior to World War I, the U.S. Army considered the symptoms of battle fatigue to be cowardice or attempts to avoid combat duty. Soldiers who reported these symptoms received harsh treatment.[243] At the time of the incidents, the two soldiers Patton slapped were believed to be suffering from "battle fatigue," otherwise known as "shell shock" or "battle stress." Today, this condition is characterized as a form of post-traumatic stress disorder, which can result from prolonged severe exposure to death and destruction, among many other traumatic events.[244] While the causes, symptoms, and effects of the condition were familiar to physicians by the time of the two incidents, it was generally less understood in military circles.[243]

An important lesson from the Tunisia Campaign was that neuropsychiatric casualties had to be treated as soon as possible and not evacuated from the combat zone. This was not done in the early stages of the Sicilian Campaign, and large numbers of neuropsychiatric casualties were evacuated to North Africa, with the result that treatment became complicated and only 15 percent of them were returned to duty. As the campaign wore on, the system became better organized and nearly 50 percent were restored to combat duty.[245]

Some time before what would become known as the "slapping incident," Patton spoke with Major General Clarence R. Huebner, the newly appointed commander of the U.S. 1st Infantry Division, in which the soldiers both served. Patton had asked Huebner for a status report; Huebner replied: "The front lines seem to be thinning out. There seems to be a very large number of 'malingerers' at the hospitals, feigning illness in order to avoid combat duty."[246] For his part, Patton did not believe the condition was real. In a directive issued to commanders on 5 August, he forbade "battle fatigue" in the Seventh Army:[247]

<templatestyles src="Template:Quote/styles.css"/>

It has come to my attention that a very small number of soldiers are going to the hospital on the pretext that they are nervously incapable of combat. Such men are cowards and bring discredit on the army and disgrace to their comrades, whom they heartlessly leave to endure the dangers of battle while they, themselves, use the hospital as a means of escape. You will take measures to see that such cases are not sent to the hospital but dealt with in

*their units. Those who are not willing to fight will be tried by court-martial
for cowardice in the face of the enemy.*

—*Patton directive to the Seventh Army, 5 August 1943*[247]

Incidents

3 August

Private Charles H. Kuhl, of L Company, U.S. 26th Infantry Regiment, reported to an aid station of C Company, 1st Medical Battalion, on 2 August
1943. Kuhl, who had been in the U.S. Army for eight months, had been attached to the 1st Infantry Division since 2 June 1943.[248] He was diagnosed
with "exhaustion," a diagnosis he had been given three times since the start of
the campaign. From the aid station, he was evacuated to a medical company
and given sodium amytal. Notes in his medical chart indicated "psychoneuro-
sis anxiety state, moderately severe (soldier has been twice before in hospital
within ten days. He can't take it at the front, evidently. He is repeatedly returned.)"[249] Kuhl was transferred from the aid station to the 15th Evacuation
Hospital near Nicosia for further evaluation.[249]

Patton arrived at the hospital the same day, accompanied by a number of medical officers, as part of his tour of the U.S. II Corps troops. He spoke to some
patients in the hospital, commending the physically wounded.[249] He then approached Kuhl, who did not appear to be physically injured.[250] Kuhl was sitting slouched on a stool midway through a tent ward filled with injured soldiers.
When Patton asked Kuhl where he was hurt, Kuhl reportedly shrugged and
replied that he was "nervous" rather than wounded, adding, "I guess I can't
take it."[251] Patton "immediately flared up,"[249] slapped Kuhl across the chin
with his gloves, then grabbed him by the collar and dragged him to the tent
entrance. He shoved him out of the tent with a kick to his backside. Yelling
"Don't admit this son of a bitch",[251] Patton demanded that Kuhl be sent back
to the front, adding, "You hear me, you gutless bastard? You're going back to
the front."[251]

Corpsmen picked up Kuhl and brought him to a ward tent, where it was discovered he had a temperature of 102.2 °F (39.0 °C);[250] and was later diagnosed
with malarial parasites. Speaking later of the incident, Kuhl noted "at the time
it happened, [Patton] was pretty well worn out ...I think he was suffering a
little battle fatigue himself."[252] Kuhl wrote to his parents about the incident,
but asked them to "just forget about it."[253] That night, Patton recorded the incident in his diary: "[I met] the only errant coward I have ever seen in this
Army. Companies should deal with such men, and if they shirk their duty,
they should be tried for cowardice and shot."[252]

Patton was accompanied in this visit by Major General John P. Lucas, who saw nothing remarkable about the incident. After the war he wrote:

There are always a certain number of such weaklings in any Army, and I suppose the modern doctor is correct in classifying them as ill and treating them as such. However, the man with malaria doesn't pass his condition on to his comrades as rapidly as does the man with cold feet nor does malaria have the lethal effect that the latter has.[254]

Patton was heard by a war correspondent angrily denying the reality of shell shock, claiming that the condition was "an invention of the Jews."

10 August

Private Paul G. Bennett, 21, of C Battery, U.S. 17th Field Artillery Regiment, was a four-year veteran of the U.S. Army, and had served in the division since March 1943. Records show he had no medical history until 6 August 1943, when a friend was wounded in combat. According to a report, he "could not sleep and was nervous."[248] Bennett was brought to the 93rd Evacuation Hospital. In addition to having a fever, he exhibited symptoms of dehydration, including fatigue, confusion, and listlessness. His request to return to his unit was turned down by medical officers.[248]

The shells going over him bothered him. The next day he was worried about his buddy and became more nervous. He was sent down to the rear echelon by a battery aid man and there the medical aid man gave him some medicine which made him sleep, but still he was nervous and disturbed. On the next day the medical officer ordered him to be evacuated, although the boy begged not to be evacuated because he did not want to leave his unit. —A medical officer describing Bennett's condition[247]

On 10 August, Patton entered the receiving tent of the hospital, speaking to the injured there. Patton approached Bennett, who was huddled and shivering, and asked what the trouble was. "It's my nerves," Bennett responded. "I can't stand the shelling anymore."[248] Patton reportedly became enraged at him, slapping him across the face. He began yelling: "Your nerves, hell, you are just a goddamned coward. Shut up that goddamned crying. I won't have these brave men who have been shot at seeing this yellow bastard sitting here crying."[248] Patton then reportedly slapped Bennett again, knocking his helmet liner off, and ordered the receiving officer, Major Charles B. Etter,[255] not to admit him.[248] Patton then threatened Bennett, "You're going back to the front lines and you may get shot and killed, but you're going to fight. If you don't, I'll stand you up against a wall and have a firing squad kill you on purpose.

Figure 21: *General Dwight Eisenhower, commander of the Sicily invasion and Patton's superior, in 1943. Eisenhower privately criticized Patton for the incidents, but refused to remove him completely from command.*

In fact, I ought to shoot you myself, you goddamned whimpering coward."[256] Upon saying this, Patton pulled out his pistol threateningly, prompting the hospital's commander, Colonel Donald E. Currier, to physically separate the two. Patton left the tent, yelling to medical officers to send Bennett back to the front lines.[256]

As he toured the remainder of the hospital, Patton continued discussing Bennett's condition with Currier. Patton stated, "I can't help it, it makes my blood boil to think of a yellow bastard being babied,"[256] and "I won't have those cowardly bastards hanging around our hospitals. We'll probably have to shoot them some time anyway, or we'll raise a breed of morons."[256]

Aftermath

Private reprimand and apologies

The 10 August incident—particularly the sight of Patton threatening a subordinate with a pistol—upset many of the medical staff present. The II Corps surgeon, Colonel Richard T. Arnest, submitted a report on the incident to Brigadier General William B. Kean, chief of staff of II Corps, who submitted it to Lieutenant General Omar Bradley, commander of II Corps. Bradley, out of loyalty to Patton, did nothing more than lock the report in his safe.[256] Arnest also sent the report through medical channels to Brigadier General Frederick A. Blesse, General Surgeon of Allied Force Headquarters, who then submitted it to Eisenhower, who received it on 16 August.[257] Eisenhower ordered Blesse to proceed immediately to Patton's command to ascertain the truth of the allegations.[255] Eisenhower also formulated a delegation to investigate the incidents from the soldiers' points of view, including Major General John P. Lucas, two colonels from the Inspector General's office, and a theater medical consultant, Lieutenant Colonel Perrin H. Long, to investigate the incident and interview those involved.[258] Long interviewed medical personnel who witnessed each incident, then filed a report entitled "Mistreatment of Patients in Receiving Tents of the 15th and 93rd Evacuation Hospitals"[256] which extensively detailed Patton's actions at both hospitals.[250]

By 18 August, Eisenhower had ordered that Patton's Seventh Army be broken up, with a few of its units remaining garrisoned in Sicily. The majority of its combat forces would be transferred to the Fifth United States Army under Lieutenant General Mark W. Clark. This had already been planned by Eisenhower, who had previously told Patton that his Seventh Army would not be part of the upcoming Allied invasion of Italy, scheduled for September.[259] On 20 August, Patton received a cable from Eisenhower regarding the arrival of Lucas at Palermo. Eisenhower told Patton it was "highly important" that he personally meet with Lucas as soon as possible, as Lucas would be carrying an important message.[260] Before Lucas arrived, Blesse arrived from Algiers to look into the health of the troops in Sicily. He was also ordered by Eisenhower to deliver a secret letter to Patton and investigate its allegations. In the letter, Eisenhower told Patton he had been informed of the slapping incidents. He said he would not be opening a formal investigation into the matter, but his criticism of Patton was sharp.[261]

<templatestyles src="Template:Quote/styles.css"/>

I clearly understand that firm and drastic measures are at times necessary in order to secure the desired objectives. But this does not excuse brutality, abuse of the sick, nor exhibition of uncontrollable temper in front of subordinates. ...I feel that the personal services you have rendered the United States and the Allied cause during the past weeks are of incalculable value; but nevertheless if there is a very considerable element of truth in the allegations accompanying this letter, I must so seriously question your good judgment and your self-discipline as to raise serious doubts in my mind as to your future usefulness. — Eisenhower's letter to Patton, dated 17 August 1943[261]

Eisenhower noted that no formal record of the incidents would be retained at Allied Headquarters, save in his own secret files. Still, he strongly suggested Patton apologize to all involved.[249,257] On 21 August, Patton brought Bennett into his office; he apologized and the men shook hands.[262] On 22 August, he met with Currier as well as the medical staff who had witnessed the events in each unit and expressed regret for his "impulsive actions." Patton related to the medical staff a story of a friend from World War I who had committed suicide after "skulking"; he stated he sought to prevent any recurrence of such an event. On 23 August, he brought Kuhl into his office, apologized, and shook hands with him as well.[263] After the apology, Kuhl said he thought Patton was "a great general," and that "at the time, he didn't know how sick I was."[263] Currier later said Patton's remarks sounded like "no apology at all, an attempt to justify what he had done."[263] Patton wrote in his diary that he loathed making the apologies, particularly when he was told by Bennett's brigade commander, Brigadier General John A. Crane, that Bennett had gone absent without leave (AWOL) and arrived at the hospital by "falsely representing his condition."[262] Patton wrote, "It is rather a commentary on justice when an Army commander has to soft-soap a skulker to placate the timidity of those above."[262] As word of the actions had spread informally among troops of the Seventh Army, Patton drove to each division under his command between 24 and 30 August and gave a 15-minute speech in which he praised their behavior and apologized for any instances where he had been too harsh on soldiers, making only vague reference to the two slapping incidents.[264] In his final apology speech to the U.S. 3rd Infantry Division, Patton was overcome with emotion when the soldiers supportively began to chant "No, general, no, no," to prevent him from having to apologize.[265]

In a letter to General George Marshall on 24 August, Eisenhower praised Patton's exploits as commander of the Seventh Army and his conduct of the Sicily campaign, particularly his ability to take initiative as a commander. Still, Eisenhower noted Patton continued "to exhibit some of those unfortunate traits of which you and I have always known."[266] He informed Marshall of the two incidents and his requirement that Patton apologize. Eisenhower stated he believed Patton would cease his behavior "because fundamentally, he is so avid for recognition as a great military commander that he will ruthlessly suppress any habit of his that will tend to jeopardize it."[264] When Eisenhower arrived in Sicily to award Montgomery the Legion of Merit on 29 August, Patton gave him a letter expressing his remorse about the incidents.[267]

Media attention

Word of the slapping incidents spread informally among soldiers before eventually circulating to war correspondents. One of the nurses who witnessed the 10 August incident apparently told her boyfriend, a captain in the Seventh Army public affairs detachment. Through him, a group of four journalists covering the Sicily operation heard of the incident, among them Demaree Bess of the *Saturday Evening Post*, Merrill Mueller of NBC News, Al Newman of *Newsweek*, and John Charles Daly of CBS News. The four journalists interviewed Etter and other witnesses, but decided to bring the matter to Eisenhower instead of filing the story with their editors. Bess, Mueller, and Quentin Reynolds of *Collier's Magazine* flew from Sicily to Algiers, and on 19 August Bess gave a summary on the slapping incidents to Eisenhower's chief of staff, Major General Walter Bedell Smith.[255] The reporters asked Eisenhower directly about the incident, and Eisenhower requested that the story be suppressed because the war effort could not afford to lose Patton. Bess and other journalists initially complied.[257] However, the news reporters then demanded Eisenhower fire Patton in exchange for them not reporting the story, a demand which Eisenhower refused.[255]

The story of Kuhl's slapping broke in the U.S. when newspaper columnist Drew Pearson revealed it on his 21 November radio program.[268] Pearson received details of the Kuhl incident and other material on Patton from his friend Ernest Cuneo, an official with the Office of Strategic Services, who obtained the information from War Department files and correspondence.[269] Pearson's version not only conflated details of both slapping incidents but falsely reported that the private in question was visibly "out of his head", telling Patton to "duck down or the shells would hit him" and that in response "Patton struck the soldier, knocking him down."[270] Pearson punctuated his broadcast by twice stating that Patton would never again be used in combat, despite the fact that Pearson had no factual basis for this prediction.[270,271] In response, Allied Headquarters denied that Patton had received an official reprimand, but confirmed that Patton had slapped at least one soldier.[272]

Patton's wife, Beatrice Patton, spoke to the media to defend him. She appeared in *True Confessions*, a women's confession magazine, where she characterized Patton as "the toughest, most hard boiled General in the U.S. Army ...but he's quite sweet, really."[273] She was featured in a *Washington Post* article on 26 November. While she did not attempt to justify Patton's action, she characterized him as a "tough perfectionist," stating that he cared deeply about the men under his command and would not ask them to do something he would not do himself.[274]

<templatestyles src="Template:Quote/styles.css"/>

He had been known to weep at men's graves—as well as tear their hides off. The deed is done and the mistake made, and I'm sure Georgie is sorrier and has punished himself more than anyone could possibly realize. I've known George Patton for 31 years and I've never known him to be deliberately unfair. He's made mistakes—and he's paid for them. This was a big mistake, and he's paying a big price for it. —Beatrice Patton in the *Washington Post, 26 November 1943*[273]

Public response

Demands for Patton to be relieved of duty and sent home were made in Congress and in newspapers across the country.[268,272] U.S. Representative Jed Johnson of Oklahoma's 6th district described Patton's actions as a "despicable incident" and was "amazed and chagrined" Patton was still in command. He called for the general's immediate dismissal on the grounds that his actions rendered him no longer useful to the war effort.[275] Representative Charles B. Hoeven of Iowa's 9th district said on the House floor that parents of soldiers need no longer worry of their children being abused by "hard boiled officers". He wondered whether the Army had "too much blood and guts."[273] Eisenhower submitted a report to Secretary of War Henry L. Stimson, who presented it to Senator Robert R. Reynolds, Chairman of the Senate Committee on Military Affairs. The report laid out Eisenhower's response to the incident and gave details of Patton's decades of military service. Eisenhower concluded that Patton was invaluable to the war effort and that he was confident the corrective actions taken would be adequate. Investigators Eisenhower sent to Patton's command found the general remained overwhelmingly popular with his troops.[276]

By mid-December, the government had received around 1,500 letters related to Patton, with many calling for his dismissal and others defending him or calling for his promotion.[275] Kuhl's father, Herman F. Kuhl, wrote to his own congressman, stating that he forgave Patton for the incident and requesting that he not be disciplined.[277] Retired generals also weighed in on the matter. Former Army Chief of Staff Charles P. Summerall wrote to Patton that he was "indignant about the publicity given a trifling incident", adding that "whatever [Patton] did" he was sure it was "justified by the provocation. Such cowards used to be shot, now they are only encouraged."[278] Major General Kenyon A. Joyce, another combat commander and one of Patton's friends, attacked Pearson as a "sensation mongerer," stating that "niceties" should be left for "softer times of peace."[279] In one notable dissension, Patton's friend, former mentor and General of the Armies John J. Pershing publicly condemned his actions, an act that left Patton "deeply hurt" and caused him to never speak to Pershing again.[274]

After consulting with Marshall, Stimson, and Assistant Secretary of War John J. McCloy,[280] Eisenhower retained Patton in the European theater, though his Seventh Army saw no further combat. Patton remained in Sicily for the rest of the year. Marshall and Stimson not only supported Eisenhower's decision, but defended it. In a letter to the U.S. Senate, Stimson stated that Patton must be retained because of the need for his "aggressive, winning leadership in the bitter battles which are to come before final victory."[281] Stimson acknowledged retaining Patton was a poor move for public relations but remained confident it was the right decision militarily.[275]

Effect on plans for invasion of Europe

Contrary to his statements to Patton, Eisenhower never seriously considered removing the general from duty in the European Theater. Writing of the incident before the media attention, he said, "If this thing ever gets out, they'll be howling for Patton's scalp, and that will be the end of Georgie's service in this war. I simply cannot let that happen. Patton is indispensable to the war effort – one of the guarantors of our victory."[255] Still, following the capture of Messina in August 1943, Patton did not command a force in combat for 11 months.[282]

Patton was passed over to lead the invasion in northern Europe. In September, Bradley—Patton's junior in both rank and experience—was selected to command the First United States Army that was forming in England to prepare for Operation Overlord.[283] According to Eisenhower, this decision had been made months before the slapping incidents became public knowledge, but Patton felt they were the reason he was denied the command.[284] Eisenhower had already decided on Bradley because he felt the invasion of Europe was too important to risk any uncertainty. While Eisenhower and Marshall both considered Patton to be a superb corps-level combat commander, Bradley possessed two of the traits that a theater-level strategic command required, and that Patton conspicuously lacked: a calm, reasoned demeanor, and a meticulously consistent nature. The slapping incidents had only further confirmed to Eisenhower that Patton lacked the ability to exercise discipline and self-control at such a command level.[242] Still, Eisenhower re-emphasized his confidence in Patton's skill as a ground combat commander by recommending him for promotion to four-star general in a private letter to Marshall on 8 September, noting his previous combat exploits and admitting that he had a "driving power" that Bradley lacked.[285]

By mid-December, Eisenhower had been appointed Supreme Allied Commander in Europe and moved to England. As media attention surrounding the

Figure 22: *Omar Bradley, whom Eisenhower selected to lead the US ground forces on the invasion of Normandy over Patton. Bradley, Patton's former subordinate, would become Patton's superior in the final months of the war.*

incident began to subside, McCloy told Patton he would indeed be eventually returning to combat command.[286] Patton was briefly considered to lead the Seventh Army in Operation Dragoon, but Eisenhower felt his experience would be more useful in the Normandy campaign.[287] Eisenhower and Marshall privately agreed that Patton would command a follow-on field army after Bradley's army conducted the initial invasion of Normandy; Bradley would then command the resulting army group. Patton was told on 1 January 1944 only that he would be relieved of command of the Seventh Army and moved to Europe. In his diary, he wrote that he would resign if he was not given command of a field army.[288] On 26 January 1944, formally given command of a newly arrived unit, the Third United States Army, he went to the United Kingdom to prepare the unit's inexperienced soldiers for combat.[289,290] This duty occupied Patton throughout early 1944.[291]

Exploiting Patton's situation, Eisenhower sent him on several high-profile trips throughout the Mediterranean in late 1943.[292] He traveled to Algiers, Tunis, Corsica, Cairo, Jerusalem, and Malta in an effort to confuse German commanders as to where the Allied forces might next attack.[268] By the next year, the German High Command still had more respect for Patton than for any other Allied commander and considered him central to any plan to invade Europe from the north.[293] Because of this, Patton was made a central figure in Operation Fortitude in early 1944.[294] The Allies fed the German intelligence organizations, through double agents, a steady stream of false intelligence that Patton had been named commander of the First United States Army Group (FUSAG) and was preparing for an invasion of Pas de Calais. The FUSAG command was actually an intricately constructed "phantom" army of decoys, props and radio signals based around southeast England to mislead German aircraft and to make Axis leaders believe a large force was massing there. Patton was ordered to keep a low profile to deceive the Germans into thinking he was in Dover throughout early 1944, when he was actually training the Third Army.[293] As a result of Operation Fortitude, the German 15th Army remained at Pas de Calais to defend against the expected attack.[295] The formation remained there even after the invasion of Normandy on 6 June 1944. Patton and the Third Army traveled to Europe and entered combat in July.[296]

References

Sources

<templatestyles src="Template:Refbegin/styles.css" />

- Atkinson, Rick (2007), *The Day of Battle: The War in Sicily and Italy, 1943–1944*, The Liberation Trilogy, New York City, New York: Henry Holt and Company, ISBN 978-0-8050-6289-2
- Axelrod, Alan (2006), *Patton: A Biography*, London, United Kingdom: Palgrave Macmillan, ISBN 978-1-4039-7139-5
- Blumenson, Martin (1974), *The Patton Papers: 1940–1945*, Boston, Massachusetts: Houghton Mifflin, ISBN 0-395-18498-3
- D'Este, Carlo (1995), *Patton: A Genius for War*, New York City, New York: Harper Collins, ISBN 0-06-016455-7
- D'Este, Carlo (2002), *Eisenhower: A Soldier's Life*, New York City, New York: Henry Holt and Company, ISBN 978-0-8050-5687-7
- Edey, Maitland A. (1968), *Time Capsule 1943*, London, United Kingdom: Littlehampton Book Services, ISBN 978-0-7054-0270-5
- Garland, Albert N.; Smyth, Howard McGaw (1965), "Sicily and the Surrender of Italy", *United States Army in World War II: The War in the Mediterranean*, Washington, D.C.: United States Army Center of Military History, US Department of the Army, OCLC 396186[297]
- Hirshson, Stanley (2003), *General Patton: A Soldier's Life*, New York City, New York: Harper Perennial, ISBN 978-0-06-000983-0
- Nimmo, Dan D.; Newsome, Chevelle, (1997), *Political Commentators In The United States In The 20th Century: a Biocritical Sourcebook*, Westport, Connecticut: Greenwood Press, ISBN 0-313-29585-9

- Province, Charles M. (2009), *The Unknown Patton*, New York City, New York: CMP Publications, ISBN 978-1-4421-5925-9
- Sweeney, Michael S. (2000), *Secrets Of Victory: The Office Of Censorship And The American Press And Radio In World War II*, Chapel Hill, North Carolina: University of North Carolina Press, ISBN 978-0-8078-4914-9
- Walker, Paul D. (2008), *Battle Fatigue: Understanding PTSD and Finding a Cure*, Bloomington, Indiana: iUniverse, ISBN 978-0-595-52996-4
- Wiltse, Charles M. (1965), "The Medical Department: Medical Service in the Mediterranean and Minor Theaters", *United States Army in World War II: The Technical Services*, Washington, D.C.: United States Army Center of Military History, US Department of the Army, OCLC 25414402[298]

Service summary of George S. Patton

Service summary of George S. Patton

George S. Patton served as a commissioned officer in the United States Army for 36 years. He served in three major conflicts (Mexican Punitive Expedition, World War I and World War II) during his military career.

Major assignments

- 15th Cavalry, Fort Sheridan, Illinois - June 1909
- 15th Cavalry, Fort Myer, Virginia - Late 1911
- Member, United States Olympic Team - Summer 1912
- Master of the Sword, Mounted Service School, Fort Riley, Kansas - September 1913 to June 1915
- Troop A, 8th Cavalry, Fort Bliss, Texas - c. July 1915 to April 1916
- Troop C, 13th Cavalry - April 1916 to May 1916
- 10th Cavalry - May 23, 1916 to May 15, 1917
- Aide to Commanding General, AEF Headquarters - May 15, 1917 to September 1917
- Commanding Officer, Headquarters Company, AEF - September 1917 to November 10, 1917
- Commanding Officer, AEF Light Tank School – November 10, 1917 to August 1918
- Commanding Officer, 1st Provisional Tank Brigade – August 1918 to November 6, 1918
- Commanding Officer, 304th Tank Brigade – November 6, 1918 to September 30, 1920
- Commanding Officer, 3rd Squadron, 3rd Cavalry – September 30, 1920 to November 20, 1922

- Student officer, Advanced Class, Cavalry School, Jan. 1, 1922, to June 6, 1923
- Student officer, General Service Schools, Sept. 12, 1923, to June 12, 1924 (Honor Graduate)
- Assistant Chief of Staff, G-1, 1st Corps Area, July, 1924, to Mar. 4, 1925
- Assistant Chief of Staff, G-1-2-3, Hawaiian Division and Hawaiian Dept., Apr., 1925, to Apr., 1928
- Office, Chief of Cavalry, Plans and Training, Apr. 14, 1928, to Aug. 17, 1931
- Student officer, Army War College, Aug. 18, 1931, to June 25, 1932
- Executive Officer, 3d Cavalry, June 25, 1932 to April 15, 1935
- Assistant Chief of Staff, G-2, Hawaiian Department, May 21, 1935 to July 12, 1937
- Director of Instruction, Cavalry School, August, 1937 to July, 1938
- Commanding Officer, 5th Cavalry Regiment, July 24, 1938 to December 1938
- Commanding Officer, 3rd Cavalry Regiment, December 1938 to July 16, 1940
- Commanding Officer, 2nd Brigade, 2nd Armored Division, July 16, 1940 to April 4, 1941
- Commanding Officer (acting), 2nd Armored Division, November, 1940 to April 4, 1941
- Commanding Officer, 2nd Armored Division, April 4, 1941 (acting since November 1940) to January 15, 1942
- Commanding Officer, I Armored Corps, January 15, 1942 – March 5, 1943
- Commanding Officer, II Corps – March 5, 1943 to April 16, 1943
- Commanding Officer, I Armored Corps, April 16, 1943 to July 9, 1943
- Commanding Officer, 7th Army, July 9, 1943 – January 26, 1944
- Commanding Officer, 1st U.S. Army Group (ficticious), January 26, 1944 to June 6, 1944
- Commanding Officer, 3rd Army, January 26, 1944 to October 7, 1945
- Military Governor of Bavaria, July 1945 to October 7, 1945
- Commanding Officer, 15th Army, October 7, 1945 to December 21, 1945

Orders, decorations and medals

Distinguished Service Cross

1st award - 26 September 1918;

CITATION: The President of the United States of America, authorized by Act of Congress, July 9, 1918, takes pleasure in presenting the Distinguished Service Cross to Colonel (Armor) George Smith Patton, Jr. (ASN: 0-2605), United States Army, for extraordinary heroism in action while serving with Tank Corps, A.E.F., near Cheppy, France, 26 September 1918. Colonel Patton displayed conspicuous courage, coolness, energy, and intelligence in directing the advance of his brigade down the valley of the Aire. Later he rallied a force of disorganized infantry and led it forward, behind the tanks, under heavy machine-gun and artillery fire until he was wounded. Unable to advance further, Colonel Patton continued to direct the operations of his unit until all arrangements for turning over the command were completed.

General Orders: War Department, General Orders No. 133 (1918)

2nd award - 19 August 1943;

SYNOPSIS: Lieutenant General George Smith Patton, Jr. (ASN: 0-2605), United States Army, was awarded a Bronze Oak Leaf Cluster in lieu of a Second Award of the Distinguished Service Cross for extraordinary heroism in connection with military operations against an armed enemy while serving as Commanding General of the 7th Army, in action against enemy forces on 11 July 1943. Lieutenant General Patton's intrepid actions, personal bravery and zealous devotion to duty exemplify the highest traditions of the military forces of the United States and reflect great credit upon himself, the 7th Army, and the United States Army.

General Orders: Headquarters, U.S. Army-North African Theater of Operations, General Orders No. 80

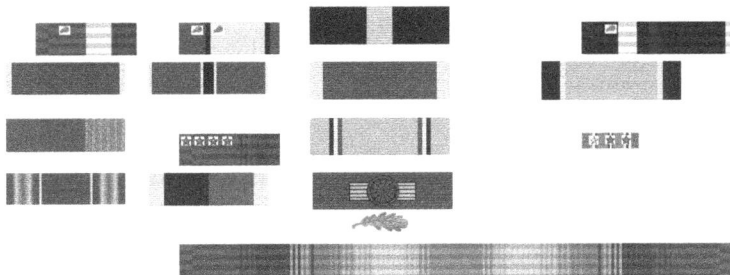

1st Row	Distinguished Service Cross with one oak leaf cluster	Army Distinguished Service Medal with two oak leaf clusters	Navy Distinguished Service Medal	Silver Star with one oak leaf cluster
2nd Row	Legion of Merit	Bronze Star Medal	Purple Heart	Silver Lifesaving Medal
3rd Row	Mexican Border Service Medal	World War I Victory Medal with four bronze campaign stars	American Defense Service Medal	European-African-Middle Eastern Campaign Medal with one silver and two bronze campaign stars
4th Row	World War II Victory Medal	Army of Occupation Medal with "Germany" clasp (posthumous)	Grand Officer of the Order of Leopold with palm (*Belgium*)	Croix de Guerre with palm (*Belgium*)
5th Row	Military Order of the White Lion, Grand cross (*Czechoslavakia*)	Czechoslovak War Cross 1939-1945	Grand Officer of the Legion of Honor (*France*)	Croix de Guerre, 1914–1918 with bronze star (*France*)
6th Row	Croix de Guerre, 1939–1945 with palm (*France*)	French Liberation Medal (1947) (posthumous)	Grand Cross of the Order of Adolphe of Nassau (*Luxembourg*)	Luxembourg War Cross
7th Row	Grand Cross of Ouissam Alaouite (*Morocco*)	Order of Kutuzov (1st class) (*Russia*)	British Honorary Knight Commander of the Order of the Bath	Honorary Knight Commander of the Order of the British Empire (KBE)

- Note: The rows 1-4 are American medals unless otherwise noted. Rows 5-7 are foreign medals and noted where required.

Dates of rank

Insignia	Rank	Component	Date
No insignia	Cadet	United States Military Academy	July 1, 1905
No insignia in 1909	Second Lieutenant	15th Cavalry, Regular Army	June 11, 1909
	First Lieutenant	10th Cavalry, Regular Army	May 23, 1916
	Captain	Cavalry, Regular Army	May 15, 1917
	Major	Cavalry, Temporary	January 26, 1918
	Lieutenant Colonel	Tank Corps, National Army	April 3, 1918[299]
	Colonel	Tank Corps, Regular Army	October 17, 1918
	Captain	Cavalry, Regular Army	June 30, 1920 (Discharged and recommissioned.)
	Major	Cavalry, Regular Army	July 1, 1920
	Lieutenant Colonel	Cavalry, Regular Army	March 1, 1934
	Colonel	Cavalry, Regular Army	July 24, 1938
	Brigadier General	Army of the United States	October 2, 1940
	Major General	Army of the United States	April 4, 1941
	Lieutenant General	Army of the United States	March 12, 1943
	Brigadier General	Regular Army (by-passed)	August 16, 1944[300]

	Major General	Regular Army	August 16, 1944[301]
	Lieutenant General	Regular Army	December 4, 1944
	General	Army of the United States	April 14, 1945

302

George S. Patton's speech to the Third Army

George S. Patton's speech to the Third Army

Patton's Speech to the Third Army was a series of speeches given by General George S. Patton to troops of the United States Third Army in 1944, prior to the Allied invasion of France. The speeches were intended to motivate the inexperienced Third Army for its pending combat duty. In the speeches, Patton urged his soldiers to do their duty regardless of personal fear, and he exhorted them to aggressiveness and constant offensive action. Patton's profanity-laced speaking was viewed as unprofessional by some other officers but the speech resounded well with his men. Some historians have acclaimed the oration as one of the greatest motivational speeches of all time.

An abbreviated and less profane version of the speech became iconic thanks to the 1970 movie *Patton*, where it was performed by the actor George C. Scott while standing before an enormous American flag. The performance was instrumental in bringing Patton into popular culture and transforming him into a folk hero.

Background

In June 1944, Lieutenant General George S. Patton was given command of the Third United States Army, a field army which was newly arrived in the United Kingdom and which was composed largely of inexperienced troops. Patton's job had been to train the Third Army to prepare it for the upcoming Allied invasion of France, where it would join in the Operation *Cobra* breakout

Figure 23: *George S. Patton as a lieutenant general*

Figure 24: *Patton speaking before a division of
the U.S. Army on 1 April 1944 in Northern Ireland*

into Brittany seven weeks after the Operation *Overlord* amphibious invasion at Normandy.[303,304]

By 1944, Patton had been established as a highly effective and successful leader, noted for his ability to inspire his men with charismatic speeches, which he delivered from memory because of a lifelong trouble with reading.[305] Patton deliberately cultivated a flashy, distinctive image in the belief that this would inspire his troops. He carried a trademark ivory-handled, Smith & Wesson Model 27 .357 Magnum.[306,307] He was usually seen wearing a highly polished helmet, riding pants, and high cavalry boots.[308] His jeep bore oversized rank placards on the front and back, as well as a klaxon horn which would loudly announce his approach from afar.[309] Patton was an effective combat commander, having rehabilitated the U.S. II Corps during the North African Campaign and then led the Seventh United States Army through the Invasion of Sicily during 1943, at times personally appearing to his troops in the middle of battle in hopes of inspiring them.[310] Patton's army had beaten British general Bernard Law Montgomery to Messina which gained him considerable fame,[311] although the infamous "slapping incident" sidelined his career for several months thereafter.[312,313]

At the time of the speeches, Patton was attempting to keep a low profile among the press, as he had been ordered to by General Dwight Eisenhower. Patton was made a central figure in an elaborate phantom army deception scheme, and the Germans believed he was in Dover preparing the (fictitious) First United States Army Group for an invasion of Pas de Calais.[314,315] On each occasion, he would wear his polished helmet, full dress uniform, and gleaming riding boots, and carry a riding crop to snap for effect. Patton frequently kept his face in a scowl he referred to as his "war face".[316] He would arrive in a Mercedes and deliver his remarks on a raised platform surrounded by a very large audience seated around the platform and on surrounding hills. Each address was delivered to a major general-led division-sized force of 15,000 or more men.[317]

The speech

Patton began delivering speeches to his troops in the United Kingdom in February 1944. The extent of his giving the particular speech that became famous is unclear, with different sources saying it had taken this form by March, or around early May,[318,319] or in late May.[316] The number of speeches given is also not clear, with one source saying four to six,[316] and others suggesting that every unit in the Third Army heard an instance.[319] The most famous and well known of the speeches occurred on 5 June 1944, the day before D-Day.[320] Though he was unaware of the actual date for the beginning of the invasion of

Europe (as the Third Army was not part of the initial landing force),[316] Patton used the speech as a motivational device to excite the men under his command and prevent them from losing their nerve.[321] Patton delivered the speech without notes, and so though it was substantially the same at each occurrence, the order of some of its parts varied.[322] One notable difference occurred in the speech he delivered on 31 May 1944, while addressing the U.S. 6th Armored Division, when he began with a remark that would later be among his most famous:[323]

<templatestyles src="Template:Quote/styles.css"/>

> No bastard ever won a war by dying for his country. He won it by making the other poor dumb bastard die for his country.[323]

Patton's words were later written down by a number of troops who witnessed his remarks, and so a number of iterations exist with differences in wording.[322] Historian Terry Brighton constructed a full speech from a number of soldiers who recounted the speech in their memoirs, including Gilbert R. Cook, Hobart R. Gay, and a number of other junior soldiers.[322] Patton only wrote briefly of his orations in his diary, noting, "as in all of my talks, I stressed fighting and killing."[321] The speech later became so popular that it was called simply "Patton's speech" or "The speech" when referencing the general.[321,316]

<templatestyles src="Template:Quote/styles.css"/>

> Be seated.
> Men, all this stuff you hear about America not wanting to fight, wanting to stay out of the war, is a lot of bullshit. Americans love to fight. All real Americans love the sting and clash of battle. When you were kids, you all admired the champion marble shooter, the fastest runner, the big-league ball players and the toughest boxers. Americans love a winner and will not tolerate a loser. Americans play to win all the time. That's why Americans have never lost and will never lose a war. The very thought of losing is hateful to Americans. Battle is the most significant competition in which a man can indulge. It brings out all that is best and it removes all that is base.
> You are not all going to die. Only two percent of you right here today would be killed in a major battle. Every man is scared in his first action. If he says he's not, he's a goddamn liar. But the real hero is the man who fights even though he's scared. Some men will get over their fright in a minute under fire, some take an hour, and for some it takes days. But the real man never lets his fear of death overpower his honor, his sense of duty to his country, and his innate manhood.
> All through your army career you men have bitched about what you call 'this chicken-shit drilling.' That is all for a purpose—to ensure instant

obedience to orders and to create constant alertness. This must be bred into every soldier. I don't give a fuck for a man who is not always on his toes. But the drilling has made veterans of all you men. You are ready! A man has to be alert all the time if he expects to keep on breathing. If not, some German son-of-a-bitch will sneak up behind him and beat him to death with a sock full of shit. There are four hundred neatly marked graves in Sicily, all because one man went to sleep on the job—but they are German graves, because we caught the bastard asleep before his officer did.

An army is a team. It lives, eats, sleeps, and fights as a team. This individual hero stuff is bullshit. The bilious bastards who write that stuff for the Saturday Evening Post don't know any more about real battle than they do about fucking. And we have the best team—we have the finest food and equipment, the best spirit and the best men in the world. Why, by God, I actually pity these poor bastards we're going up against.

All the real heroes are not storybook combat fighters. Every single man in the army plays a vital role. So don't ever let up. Don't ever think that your job is unimportant. What if every truck driver decided that he didn't like the whine of the shells and turned yellow and jumped headlong into a ditch? That cowardly bastard could say to himself, 'Hell, they won't miss me, just one man in thousands.' What if every man said that? Where in the hell would we be then? No, thank God, Americans don't say that. Every man does his job. Every man is important. The ordinance men are needed to supply the guns, the quartermaster is needed to bring up the food and clothes for us because where we are going there isn't a hell of a lot to steal. Every last damn man in the mess hall, even the one who boils the water to keep us from getting the GI shits, has a job to do.

Each man must think not only of himself, but think of his buddy fighting alongside him. We don't want yellow cowards in the army. They should be killed off like flies. If not, they will go back home after the war, goddamn cowards, and breed more cowards. The brave men will breed more brave men. Kill off the goddamn cowards and we'll have a nation of brave men.

One of the bravest men I saw in the African campaign was on a telegraph pole in the midst of furious fire while we were moving toward Tunis. I stopped and asked him what the hell he was doing up there. He answered, 'Fixing the wire, sir.' 'Isn't it a little unhealthy up there right now?' I asked. 'Yes sir, but this goddamn wire has got to be fixed.' I asked, 'Don't those planes strafing the road bother you?' And he answered, 'No sir, but you sure as hell do.' Now, there was a real soldier. A real man. A man who devoted all he had to his duty, no matter how great the odds, no matter how seemingly insignificant his duty appeared at the time.

And you should have seen the trucks on the road to Gabès. Those drivers were magnificent. All day and all night they crawled along those son-of-a-bitch roads, never stopping, never deviating from their course with shells bursting all around them. Many of the men drove over 40 consecutive hours. We got through on good old American guts. These were not combat men. But they were soldiers with a job to do. They were part of a team. Without them the fight would have been lost.

Sure, we all want to go home. We want to get this war over with. But you can't win a war lying down. The quickest way to get it over with is to get the bastards who started it. We want to get the hell over there and clean the goddamn thing up, and then get at those purple-pissing Japs. The quicker they are whipped, the quicker we go home. The shortest way home is through Berlin and Tokyo. So keep moving. And when we get to Berlin, I am personally going to shoot that paper-hanging son-of-a-bitch Hitler.

When a man is lying in a shell hole, if he just stays there all day, a Boche will get him eventually. The hell with that. My men don't dig foxholes. Foxholes only slow up an offensive. Keep moving. We'll win this war, but we'll win it only by fighting and showing the Germans that we've got more guts than they have or ever will have. We're not just going to shoot the bastards, we're going to rip out their living goddamned guts and use them to grease the treads of our tanks. We're going to murder those lousy Hun cocksuckers by the bushel-fucking-basket.

Some of you men are wondering whether or not you'll chicken out under fire. Don't worry about it. I can assure you that you'll all do your duty. War is a bloody business, a killing business. The Nazis are the enemy. Wade into them, spill their blood or they will spill yours. Shoot them in the guts. Rip open their belly. When shells are hitting all around you and you wipe the dirt from your face and you realize that it's not dirt, it's the blood and gut of what was once your best friend, you'll know what to do. I don't want any messages saying 'I'm holding my position.' We're not holding a goddamned thing. We're advancing constantly and we're not interested in holding anything except the enemy's balls. We're going to hold him by his balls and we're going to kick him in the ass; twist his balls and kick the living shit out of him all the time. Our plan of operation is to advance and keep on advancing. We're going to go through the enemy like shit through a tinhorn.

There will be some complaints that we're pushing our people too hard. I don't give a damn about such complaints. I believe that an ounce of sweat will save a gallon of blood. The harder we push, the more Germans we kill. The more Germans we kill, the fewer of our men will be killed. Pushing harder means fewer casualties. I want you all to remember that.

My men don't surrender. I don't want to hear of any soldier under my command being captured unless he is hit. Even if you are hit, you can still fight. That's not just bullshit either. I want men like the lieutenant in Libya who, with a Luger against his chest, swept aside the gun with his hand, jerked his helmet off with the other and busted the hell out of the Boche with the helmet. Then he picked up the gun and he killed another German. All this time the man had a bullet through his lung. That's a man for you!

Don't forget, you don't know I'm here at all. No word of that fact is to be mentioned in any letters. The world is not supposed to know what the hell they did with me. I'm not supposed to be commanding this army. I'm not even supposed to be in England. Let the first bastards to find out be the goddamned Germans. Some day, I want them to rise up on their piss-soaked hind legs and howl 'Ach! It's the goddamned Third Army and that son-of-a-bitch Patton again!'

Then there's one thing you men will be able to say when this war is over and you get back home. Thirty years from now when you're sitting by your fireside with your grandson on your knee and he asks, 'What did you do in the great World War Two?' You won't have to cough and say, 'Well, your granddaddy shoveled shit in Louisiana.' No sir, you can look him straight in the eye and say 'Son, your granddaddy rode with the great Third Army and a son-of-a-goddamned-bitch named George Patton!'

All right, you sons of bitches. You know how I feel. I'll be proud to lead you wonderful guys in battle anytime, anywhere. That's all.[324]

Impact

The troops under Patton's command received the speech well. The general's strong reputation caused considerable excitement among his men, and they listened intently, in absolute silence, as he spoke.[317] A majority indicated they enjoyed Patton's speaking style. As one officer recounted of the end of the speech, "The men instinctively sensed the fact and the telling mark that they themselves would play in world history because of it, for they were being told as much right now. Deep sincerity and seriousness lay behind the General's colorful words, and the men well knew it, but they loved the way he put it as only he could do it."[325] Patton gave a humorous tone to the speech, as he intentionally sought to make his men laugh with his colorful delivery. Observers later noted the troops seemed to find the speeches very funny.[317] In particular, Patton's use of obscene humor was well received by the enlisted men,[326] as it was "the language of the barracks".[316]

A notable minority of Patton's officers were unimpressed or displeased with their commander's use of obscenities, viewing it as unprofessional conduct for a military officer.[321,327] Among some officers' later recounting of the speech, *bullshit* would be replaced by *baloney* and *fucking* by *fornicating*. At least one account replaced "We're going to hold the enemy by the balls" with "We're going to hold the enemy by the nose."[322] Among the critics of Patton's frequent use of vulgarities was General Omar Bradley, Patton's former subordinate.[328] It was well known that the two men were polar opposites in personality, and there is considerable evidence that Bradley disliked Patton both personally and professionally.[329] In response to criticisms of his coarse language, Patton wrote to a family member, "When I want my men to remember something important, to really make it stick, I give it to them double dirty. It may not sound nice to a bunch of little old ladies, at an afternoon tea party, but it helps my soldiers to remember. You can't run an army without profanity, and it has to be eloquent profanity. An army without profanity couldn't fight its way out of a piss-soaked paper bag."[322]

Under Patton, the Third Army landed in Normandy during July 1944 and would go on to play an integral role in the last months of the war in Europe, closing the Falaise Pocket in mid-August,[330] and playing the key role in re-lieving the siege of Bastogne during the Battle of the Bulge in December, a feat regarded as one of the most notable achievements in the war. The rapid offensive action and speed that Patton called for in the speech became actions which brought the Third Army wide acclaim in the campaign.[331]

Historians acclaim the speech as one of Patton's best works. Author Terry Brighton called it "the greatest motivational speech of the war and perhaps of all time, exceeding (in its morale boosting effect if not as literature) the words Shakespeare gave King Henry V at Agincourt."[316] Alan Axelrod contended it was the most famous of his many memorable quotes.[321]

The speech became an icon of popular culture after the 1970 film *Patton*, which was about the general's wartime exploits. The opening of the movie saw actor George C. Scott, as Patton, delivering a toned-down version of the speech before an enormous American flag.[332] It began with a version of Patton's "No bastard ever won a war by dying for his country ..." quote. Scott's iteration omitted much of the middle of the speech relating to Patton's anecdotes about Sicily and Libya, as well as his remarks about the importance of every soldier to the war effort.[326] In contrast to Patton's humorous approach, Scott delivered the speech in an entirely serious, low and gruff tone.[333] Still, Scott's depiction of Patton in this scene is an iconic depiction of the General which earned Scott an Academy Award for Best Actor, and was instrumental in bringing Patton into popular culture as a folk hero.[333]

References

Sources

<templatestyles src="Template:Refbegin/styles.css" />

- Axelrod, Alan (2006), *Patton: A Biography*, London, United Kingdom: Palgrave Macmillan, ISBN 978-1-4039-7139-5
- Blumenson, Martin (1974), *The Patton Papers: 1940–1945*, Boston, Massachusetts: Houghton Mifflin, ISBN 0-395-18498-3
- Brighton, Terry (2009), *Patton, Montgomery, Rommel: Masters of War*, Crown Publishing Group, ISBN 978-0-307-46154-4
- D'Este, Carlo (1995), *Patton: A Genius for War*, New York City, New York: Harper Collins, ISBN 0-06-016455-7
- Gist, Brenda Lovelace (2010), *Eloquently speaking*, Bloomington, Indiana: Xlibris, ISBN 978-1456811525
- Zaloga, Steven (2010), *George S. Patton: Leadership, Strategy, Conflict*, Oxford, United Kingdom: Osprey Publishing, ISBN 978-1846034596

<indicator name="good-star"> ⊕ </indicator>

Appendix

References

[1] D'Este 1995, p. 29.
[2] Brighton 2009, p. 17.
[3] Axelrod 2006, pp. 11–12.
[4] Historians Carlo D'Este and Alan Axelrod note in their biographies of Patton that these difficulties were likely the result of undiagnosed dyslexia.<ref name="FOOTNOTEAxelrod200611–12">Axelrod 2006, pp. 11–12.
[5] Axelrod 2006, p. 13.
[6] Axelrod 2006, pp. 28, 35, 65–66.
[7] Axelrod 2006, pp. 14–15.
[8] Blumenson 1972, p. 92.
[9] Zaloga 2010, p. 7.
[10] Axelrod 2006, pp. 20–23.
[11] Brighton 2009, p. 19.
[12] Axelrod 2006, p. 24.
[13] D'Este 1995, pp. 58, 131.
[14] Rice 2004, p. 32.
[15] 21st Century Patton: Strategic Insights for the Modern Era edited by J. Furman Daniel III pg. 61
[16] D'Este 1995, p. 9.
[17] Zaloga 2010, p. 6.
[18] Bennett, Abram Elting. Huguenots migration: descendants' contributions to America. University of Wisconsin-Madison, 1984. Page 109
[19] Patton, Robert H. The Pattons: A Personal History of an American Family. 1994, pages 3-5
[20] Brighton 2009, p. 20.
[21] Axelrod 2006, pp. 26–27.
[22] Axelrod 2006, pp. 28–29.
[23] Zaloga 2010, p. 8.
[24] Axelrod 2006, p. 30.
[25] Blumenson 1972, pp. 231–234.
[26] D'Este 1995, pp. 132–133.
[27] D'Este 1995, p. 134.
[28] D'Este 1995, pp. 140–142.
[29] Axelrod 2006, pp. 31–32.
[30] D'Este 1995, p. 145.
[31] Brighton 2009, p. 21.
[32] Axelrod 2006, pp. 33–34.
[33] D'Este 1995, p. 153.
[34] Axelrod 2006, p. 35.
[35] D'Este 1995, p. 148.
[36] Jowett & de Quesada 2006, p. 25.
[37] Axelrod 2006, p. 36.
[38] D'Este 1995, pp. 158–159.
[39] Zaloga 2010, p. 9.
[40] D'Este 1995, pp. 162–163.
[41] Zaloga 2010, p. 10.
[42] D'Este 1995, p. 165.
[43] Brighton 2009, p. 31.
[44] Axelrod 2006, pp. 38–39.
[45] Axelrod 2006, p. 40.
[46] Axelrod 2006, pp. 41–42.

[47] D'Este 1995, pp. 172–175.
[48] Brighton 2009, p. 32.
[49] Axelrod 2006, p. 43.
[50] Axelrod 2006, p. 46.
[51] Axelrod 2006, p. 47.
[52] Axelrod 2006, pp. 47–48.
[53] Axelrod 2006, p. 49.
[54] D'Este 1995, pp. 204–208.
[55] Blumenson 1972, pp. 480–483.
[56] Blumenson 1972, pp. 552–553.
[57] Axelrod 2006, pp. 50–52.
[58] Axelrod 2006, p. 53.
[59] Blumenson 1972, pp. 661–670.
[60] Brighton 2009, p. 38.
[61] Blumenson 1972, pp. 706–708.
[62] Axelrod 2006, pp. 54–55.
[63] Axelrod 2006, pp. 56–57.
[64] Brighton 2009, p. 40.
[65] Blumenson 1972, pp. 764–766.
[66] Blumenson 1974, p. 616.
[67] Axelrod 2006, pp. 58–59.
[68] Axelrod 2006, p. 62.
[69] Axelrod 2006, pp. 63–64.
[70] Brighton 2009, p. 46.
[71] Axelrod 2006, pp. 65–66.
[72] Steele 2005, p. 18.
[73] Brighton 2009, p. 57.
[74] D'Este 1995, p. 335.
[75] Axelrod 2006, pp. 67–68.
[76] Axelrod 2006, pp. 69–70.
[77] Brighton 2009, pp. 58–59.
[78] Allen & Dickson 2006, p. 194.
[79] D'Este 1995, p. 361.
[80] Axelrod 2006, pp. 71–72.
[81] Brighton 2009, pp. 379—380.
[82] Axelrod 2006, pp. 73–74.
[83] Axelrod 2006, pp. 75–76.
[84] Brighton 2009, pp. 82–83.
[85] Axelrod 2006, pp. 77–79.
[86] Brighton 2009, p. 85.
[87] Brighton 2009, p. 106.
[88] Axelrod 2006, pp. 80–82.
[89] Axelrod 2006, p. 83.
[90] Axelrod 2006, pp. 84–85.
[91] Blumenson 1974, p. 542.
[92] Lovelace 2014, p. 110.
[93] Axelrod 2006, p. 2.
[94] Brighton 2009, pp. 117–119.
[95] Axelrod 2006, pp. 88–90.
[96] Axelrod 2006, pp. 91–93.
[97] Brighton 2009, pp. 165–166.
[98] Edey 1968, p. 60.
[99] Axelrod 2006, pp. 94.
[100] Blumenson 1985, p. 182.
[101] Axelrod 2006, pp. 96–97.
[102] Hunt 1990, p. 169.

[103] Axelrod 2006, pp. 98–99.
[104] Brighton 2009, p. 188.
[105] Axelrod 2006, pp. 101–104.
[106] Brighton 2009, pp. 201–202.
[107] Axelrod 2006, pp. 105–107.
[108] Axelrod 2006, pp. 108–109.
[109] Axelrod 2006, pp. 110–111.
[110] Brighton 2009, p. 215.
[111] Atkinson 2007, p. 119.
[112] D'Este 1995, p. 466.
[113] Blumenson 1974, p. 331.
[114] Axelrod 2006, p. 118.
[115] Axelrod 2006, p. 117.
[116] Blumenson 1974, p. 329.
[117] Blumenson 1974, p. 336.
[118] Blumenson 1974, p. 338.
[119] D'Este 1995, pp. 535–536.
[120] Axelrod 2006, p. 120.
[121] Edey 1968, pp. 160–166.
[122] Blumenson 1974, p. 379.
[123] Blumenson 1974, p. 377.
[124] D'Este 1995, p. 543.
[125] Axelrod 2006, p. 122.
[126] Blumenson 1974, p. 345.
[127] Axelrod 2006, p. 121.
[128] Blumenson 1974, p. 348.
[129] Blumenson 1974, p. 407.
[130] Axelrod 2006, p. 124.
[131] Blumenson 1974, p. 423.
[132] Axelrod 2006, p. 127.
[133] Blumenson 1974, p. 409.
[134] Axelrod 2006, p. 128.
[135] Axelrod 2006, p. 132.
[136] Patton's friend Gilbert R. Cook was his deputy commander, whom Patton later had to relieve due to illness, a decision which "shook him to the core".<ref name="FOOTNOTEEssame1974178">Essame 1974, p. 178.
[137] Axelrod 2006, p. 135–136.
[138] Axelrod 2006, pp. 139–140.
[139] Axelrod 2006, p. 137.
[140] Jarymowycz 2001, pp. 215–216.
[141] Jarymowycz 2001, pp. 212.
[142] Gooderson 1998, p. 44.
[143] Gooderson 1998, p. 85.
[144] Axelrod 2006, p. 138.
[145] Jarymowycz 2001, p. 217.
[146] Ambrose 2007, pp. 162–164.
[147] Zaloga 2008, pp. 184–193.
[148] Axelrod 2006, p. 141.
[149] von Mellenthin 2006, pp. 381–382.
[150] https://www.c-span.org/video/?68490-1/patton-genius-war
[151] Axelrod 2006, p. 142.
[152] Hirshson 2003, p. 546.
[153] D'Este 1995, p. 669.
[154] Axelrod 2006, pp. 143–144.
[155] D'Este 1995, pp. 675–678.
[156] McNeese 2003, p. 77.

[157] Blumenson 1974, p. 599.
[158] McNeese 2003, p. 75.
[159] Axelrod 2006, pp. 148–149.
[160] McNeese 2003, p. 78.
[161] McNeese 2003, p. 79.
[162] Axelrod 2006, pp. 152–153.
[163] Le Tissier 2007, pp. 147–155.
[164] Axelrod 2006, p. 156.
[165] Rickard 2004, p. 85.
[166] Regan 1992, p. 53.
[167] Axelrod 2006, p. 157.
[168] Brighton 2009, p. 322.
[169] Farago 1964, p. 790.
[170] Axelrod 2006, pp. 158–159.
[171] Blumenson 1974, p. 655.
[172] Axelrod 2006, pp. 160–162.
[173] Wallace 1946, pp. 194–195.
[174] Fuller 2004, p. 254.
[175] Blumenson 1974, p. 721.
[176] Axelrod 2006, pp. 163–164.
[177] Associated Press, "Patton Fails To Get Task in Orient", *The San Bernardino Daily Sun*, San Bernardino, California, Friday 15 June 1945, Volume 51, page 2.
[178] D'Este 1995, p. 744.
[179] Hirshson 2003, p. 535.
[180] Showalter 2006, pp. 412–13.
[181] D'Este 1995, p. 743.
[182] Axelrod 2006, pp. 165–166.
[183] Brighton 2009, p. 16.
[184] Axelrod 2006, p. 167.
[185] Farago 1964, pp. 826—827.
[186] Axelrod 2006, pp. 168–169.
[187] https//www.telegraph.co.uk summarizing Robert Wilcox's *Target Patton*; accessed July 3, 2018.
[188] Axelrod 2006, p. ix.
[189] Brighton 2009, p. xv.
[190] Axelrod 2006, p. viii.
[191] D'Este 1995, p. 1.
[192] Brighton 2009, p. xvi.
[193] D'Este 1995, p. 478.
[194] Axelrod 2006, p. 4.
[195] Brighton 2009, pp. 36–37.
[196] D'Este 1995, p. 578.
[197] Axelrod 2006, pp. 130–131.
[198] Evans 2001, pp. 151–168.
[199] Lovelace 2014, p. 111.
[200] Lovelace 2014, p. 113.
[201] Lovelace 2014, p. 114.
[202] Lovelace 2014, p. 117.
[203] D'Este 1995, pp. 467–468.
[204] Atkinson 2007, p. 147.
[205] Wallace 1946, p. 97.
[206] Brighton 2009, p. 18.
[207] Patton 1947, p. 60.
[208] Hirshson 2003, p. 864.
[209] D'Este 1995, p. 726.
[210] Patton 1947, p. 49.

[211] D'Este 1995, p. 739.
[212] D'Este 2002, p. 801.
[213] D'Este 1995, p. 818.
[214] D'Este 1995, p. 536.
[215] D'Este 2002, p. 442.
[216] D'Este 1995, pp. 466–467.
[217] D'Este 2002, pp. 403–404.
[218] DeFelice 2011, p. 402.
[219] D'Este 1995, p. 755.
[220] D'Este 1995, p. 451.
[221] D'Este 1995, p. 549.
[222] Blumenson 1974, p. 801.
[223] Hirshson 2003, p. 562.
[224] D'Este 1995, p. 815.
[225] Among the opinions of Patton's abilities, *Oberstleutnant* Horst Freiherr von Wangenheim, operations officer of the 277th Volksgrenadier Division, stated that "General Patton is the most feared general on all fronts. [His] tactics are daring and unpredictable.... He is the most modern general and the best commander of [combined] armored and infantry forces."<ref name="FOOTNOTEBlumenson1974480–483">Blumenson 1974, pp. 480–483.
[226] Brighton 2009, p. xvii.
[227] Axelrod 2006, p. 1.
[228] https://books.google.com/books?id=2mG1CwAAQBAJ
[229] http://www.vmi.edu/archives.aspx?id=5299
[230] http://www.generalpatton.org/
[231] https://web.archive.org/web/20070628163408/http://www.pattonuncovered.com/index.htm
[232] https://web.archive.org/web/20060528203232/http://www.efour4ever.com/44thdivision/bridgehead.htm
[233] http://www.nat-military-museum.lu/
[234] https://www.youtube.com/watch?v=gvL0tj9ZaoY
[235] https://archive.org/details/gov.archives.arc.2569725
[236] https://www.loc.gov/collections/george-s-patton-diaries/about-this-collection/
[237] Axelrod 2006, pp. 101–104.
[238] Axelrod 2006, pp. 105–107.
[239] Axelrod 2006, pp. 108–109.
[240] Axelrod 2006, pp. 96–97.
[241] Axelrod 2006, pp. 77–78.
[242] Blumenson 1974, p. 348.
[243] Walker 2008, p. xiv.
[244] Walker 2008, p. xv.
[245] Wiltse 1965, pp. 171–172.
[246] Province 2009, p. 26.
[247] Axelrod 2006, p. 117.
[248] Blumenson 1974, p. 331.
[249] Blumenson 1974, p. 330.
[250] Axelrod 2006, p. 115.
[251] Atkinson 2007, p. 147.
[252] Axelrod 2006, p. 116.
[253] D'Este 1995, p. 901.
[254] Garland & Smyth 1965, p. 427.
[255] D'Este 1995, pp. 535–536.
[256] Axelrod 2006, p. 118.
[257] Axelrod 2006, p. 119.
[258] D'Este 1995, p. 902.
[259] Blumenson 1974, p. 327.
[260] Blumenson 1974, p. 328.
[261] Blumenson 1974, p. 329.

[262] Blumenson 1974, p. 334.
[263] Blumenson 1974, p. 336.
[264] Blumenson 1974, p. 338.
[265] Blumenson 1974, p. 342.
[266] Blumenson 1974, p. 337.
[267] Blumenson 1974, p. 341.
[268] Axelrod 2006, p. 120.
[269] Hirshson 2003, p. 424.
[270] Sweeney 2000, p. 158.
[271] Nimmo & Newsome 1997, p. 274.
[272] Edey 1968, pp. 160–166.
[273] Blumenson 1974, p. 380.
[274] Blumenson 1974, p. 379.
[275] Blumenson 1974, p. 377.
[276] Blumenson 1974, p. 376.
[277] D'Este 1995, pp. 543–544.
[278] Blumenson 1974, p. 378.
[279] Blumenson 1974, p. 383.
[280] D'Este 2002, p. 442.
[281] D'Este 1995, p. 543.
[282] Axelrod 2006, p. 122.
[283] Blumenson 1974, p. 345.
[284] Axelrod 2006, p. 121.
[285] Blumenson 1974, p. 349.
[286] Blumenson 1974, p. 387.
[287] Blumenson 1974, p. 399.
[288] Blumenson 1974, pp. 390–394.
[289] Blumenson 1974, p. 407.
[290] Axelrod 2006, p. 124.
[291] Blumenson 1974, p. 423.
[292] Blumenson 1974, p. 366.
[293] Axelrod 2006, p. 127.
[294] Blumenson 1974, p. 409.
[295] Axelrod 2006, p. 128.
[296] Axelrod 2006, p. 132.
[297] //www.worldcat.org/oclc/396186
[298] //www.worldcat.org/oclc/25414402
[299] Official date of rank of March 20, 1918
[300] Official Date Of Rank of September 1, 1943
[301] Official Date Of Rank of September 2, 1943
[302] Official Register of Commissioned Officers of the United States Army, 1941. pg. 659.
[303] Blumenson 1974, p. 407.
[304] Axelrod 2006, p. 124.
[305] Axelrod 2006, pp. 67–68.
[306] Zaloga 2010, p. 9.
[307] Brighton 2009, p. xvi.
[308] D'Este 1995, p. 478.
[309] Axelrod 2006, pp. 77–79.
[310] Brighton 2009, pp. 201–202.
[311] Axelrod 2006, pp. 110–111.
[312] Blumenson 1974, p. 331.
[313] Axelrod 2006, p. 117.
[314] Blumenson 1974, p. 409.
[315] Axelrod 2006, p. 127.
[316] Brighton 2009, p. 260.
[317] D'Este 1995, p. 601.

[318] Blumenson 1974, p. 456.
[319] Axelrod 2006, p. 21.
[320] Gist 2010, p. 477.
[321] Axelrod 2006, pp. 130–131.
[322] Brighton 2009, p. 261.
[323] Gist 2010, p. 487.
[324] Brighton 2009, pp. 262–265.
[325] D'Este 1995, p. 604.
[326] D'Este 1995, p. 603.
[327] Brighton 2009, p. 249.
[328] D'Este 1995, p. 578.
[329] D'Este 1995, pp. 466–467.
[330] Axelrod 2006, p. 139–140.
[331] Axelrod 2006, pp. 152–153.
[332] D'Este 1995, p. 602.
[333] D'Este 1995, p. 1–2.

Article Sources and Contributors

The sources listed for each article provide more detailed licensing information including the copyright status, the copyright owner, and the license conditions.

George S. Patton *Source:* https://en.wikipedia.org/w/index.php?oldid=853674339 *License:* Creative Commons Attribution-Share Alike 3.0 *Contributors:* 1990'sguy, Absolutelypuremilk, Acroterion, Afernand74, Alfie Gandon, Anonimeco, Arjayay, ArnoldReinhold, Atchom, AustralianRupert, AvalerionV, Berean Hunter, Berserker276, Berty688, Billmckern, Binksternet, Blue Edits, Bradfranklin23, Bronze2018, BrownHairedGirl, Brutaldeluxe, C.Fred, CAPTAIN RAJU, CDarienzo, CLCStudent, Capt.J.W.King, Certes, Chewings72, Chromebook12345, Clarinetguy097, Clayton Forrester, ClueBot NG, Cobatfor, Conwaylanz, Crystallizedcarbon, Cuprum17, DHeyward, DamionT1995, Dave Dial, Dick goesinya, Dlabtot, Dlfreem, DocWatson42, DynV, Ed!, Eric-Wester, Esszet, Excirial, Favonian, Fdewaele, Firstorm, Flaffa91, Fogelstrom, GEO Graves, LLC, Gaia Octavia Agrippa, Gr8h8m8, Grammarian3.14159265359, GreenMeansGo, HaeB, Hmains, Hohum, Huberthoff, Ian Rose, Illegitimate Barrister, Imperialpref, Isaacroq, JCSantos, JSweit8573, Jablonskyman, JaguarJon53, Javert2113, Jdaloner, Jdcomix, Jim1138, Jjcoolcubes, Jmg38, Joe Vitale 5, John, John of Reading, JohnWilmerding, Johnuniq, Jwy, KConWiki, KD53, KNHaw, Kendall-K1, L3X1, Landingdude13, Laurdecl, MPS1992, Malerooster, Mark Sublette, Matuko, Mean as custard, Meatsgains, Melcous, MisfitToys, Mndata, Mojo Hand, Mosoporieot1, Mr Stephen, Mr. Guye, My Chemistry romantic, Mztourist, Narky Blert, Neptune's Trident, Ogbrewer, Oshwah, Otr500, PBS, Prenza00, Prest146, Prinsipe Ybarro, Quisqualis, RFD, Randy Kryn, Rjensen, RobertLunaIII, Rodw, Rsarlls, Samf4u, Sannuik12345, Sb2001, Serols, Shellwood, Slightsmile, Smaines, T-bonham, The Blade of the Northern Lights, The PIPE, TheDragonFire, Thewolfchild, Tobby72, Watson01, Wenhammuseum, Widr, Wikiuser100, Yamaguchi先生, Yodin, Your mom321, ZappaOMati, 146 anonymous edits   1

George S. Patton slapping incidents *Source:* https://en.wikipedia.org/w/index.php?oldid=831515041 *License:* Creative Commons Attribution-Share Alike 3.0 *Contributors:* A. Carty, Altamel, Altaïr, AmericanLemming, Another Believer, AustralianRupert, Bender235, Bgwhite, Bob Burkhardt, Bri, Buggie111, Clarityfiend, ColonelCourageous, DJ Jones74, DMorpheus2, David Fuchs, David.moreno72, Deeday-UK, Dellant, Diannaa, Dimadick, Dodgerblue777, DrKay, DragonflySixtyseven, Dweller, Ed!, Esrever, Fourthords, Gerda Arendt, Gnangarra, Good Olfactory, HandsomeFella, Hawkeye7, JackofOz, Jamie7687, Jarodalien, Jatkins, Joefromrandb, John Paul Parks, Jokestress, Julietdeltalima, KConWiki, Kablammo, Khazar2, Klemen Kocjancic, Kumioko (renamed), Laurinavicius, Logistiguru, Lotje, Mart572, Materialscientist, Midnightblueowl, Minipetty, Mr Stephen, Newzild, Niceguyedc, Nick-D, Oddbodz, Oneultralamewhiteboy, Oshwah, Paonea, RobertG, Sizeofint, Smarkflea, SteveMiamiBeach, SucreRouge, Tabletop, Tonedef1, Torqueing, Tpbradbury, Vanquisher.UA, Vintovka Dragunova, Wen D House, Wikih101, Wtmitchell, Xanzzibar, Zawed, 77 anonymous edits   43

Service summary of George S. Patton *Source:* https://en.wikipedia.org/w/index.php?oldid=849832316 *License:* Creative Commons Attribution-Share Alike 3.0 *Contributors:* Abraham, B.S., BD2412, Cnwilliams, CommonsDelinker, Ed!, EdmundT, Eleos, Evans1982, GregJackP, Illegitimate Barrister, JackofOz, McOleo, Serols, Thewolfchild, Ulric1313, 116 anonymous edits   57

George S. Patton's speech to the Third Army *Source:* https://en.wikipedia.org/w/index.php?oldid=851852270 *License:* Creative Commons Attribution-Share Alike 3.0 *Contributors:* Aa77zz, Aalox, Acroterion, Albany NY, Amortias, AnonMoos, Arjayay, Bilsonius, Bongwarrior, Budalata, Butterbur, CV9933, ClueBot NG, Cmprovince, Cramyourspam, Crazymonkey1123, Cwobeel, DadaNeem, Danhash, Dank, Dfdemt, Ed!, Enterprisey, Esrever, Fadookie, Favonian, FlickrWarrior, Fuferito, Gaarmyvet, Giraffedata, Inops, JJMC89, JaconaFrere, Jarodalien, Jmg38, Joshdboz, KaletheQuick, Kencf0618, Lancer2011, Magioladitis, Matt Deres, Mbarbier, Moonriddengirl, OpenInfoForAll, PaulHanson, Peacemaker67, Pigsonthewing, Regulov, Renegadeviking, Rickie.Moran, Slightsmile, Squids and Chips, Tim!, Timbouctou, Trilobitealive, Vanamonde93, VoABot II, Wasted Time R, Wikiuser100, Wwallacee, Xanzzibar, 44 anonymous edits   63

80

Image Sources, Licenses and Contributors

The sources listed for each image provide more detailed licensing information including the copyright status, the copyright owner, and the license conditions.

Image *Source:* https://en.wikipedia.org/w/index.php?title=File:Pattonphoto.jpg *License:* Public Domain *Contributors:* User Husnock on en.wikipedia 1

Image *Source:* https://en.wikipedia.org/w/index.php?title=File:US-O10_insignia.svg *License:* Public Domain *Contributors:* Ipankonin 2

Image *Source:* https://en.wikipedia.org/w/index.php?title=File:George_S_Patton_Signature.svg *License:* Public Domain *Contributors:* George S. Patton 2

Figure 1 *Source:* https://en.wikipedia.org/w/index.php?title=File:Nita_Patton_(Sister_of_General_George_S._Patton).jpg *Contributors:* Billmckern 4

Figure 2 *Source:* https://en.wikipedia.org/w/index.php?title=File:Patton_at_VMI_1907.jpg *License:* Public Domain *Contributors:* Banjo, BotMultichill, FieldMarine, File Upload Bot (Magnus Manske), OgreBot 2, Rodhullandemu, Väsk, 1 anonymous edits 5

Figure 3 *Source:* https://en.wikipedia.org/w/index.php?title=File:Wooltex_and_George_S_Patton.jpg *License:* Public Domain *Contributors:* Uncreditied photographer 7

Figure 4 *Source:* https://en.wikipedia.org/w/index.php?title=File:1915-dodge-archives.jpg *License:* Attribution *Contributors:* Infrogmation, MartinHansV, Meno25, Michael Barera, Morio, OgreBot 2, Undead warrior, W like wiki, WOSlinker 9

Figure 5 *Source:* https://en.wikipedia.org/w/index.php?title=File:George_S._Patton_-_France_-_1918.jpg *License:* Public Domain *Contributors:* Signal Corps 10

Figure 6 *Source:* https://en.wikipedia.org/w/index.php?title=File:George_S._Patton_1919.jpg *Contributors:* U.S. Army 12

Figure 7 *Source:* https//en.wikipedia.org *Contributors:* Catsmeat, Cobatfor, Jan Arkesteijn, John N., Martin H., Randroide~commonswiki 16

Figure 8 *Source:* https://en.wikipedia.org/w/index.php?title=File:Patton_speaking_with_Lt._Col._Lyle_Bernard,_at_Brolo,_circa_1943.jpg *License:* Public Domain *Contributors:* Army Signal Corps 18

Figure 9 *Source:* https://en.wikipedia.org/w/index.php?title=File:Wounded-on_wayto-hospital-RG-208-AA-158-A-015.jpg *License:* Public Domain *Contributors:* Ed!, Slowking4, Tm 19

Figure 10 *Source:* https//en.wikipedia.org *License:* Public Domain *Contributors:* Elinruby, Fæ, Hilohello, Howard61313, Le Passant 23

Image *Source:* https://en.wikipedia.org/w/index.php?title=File:Nuvola_apps_kaboodle.svg *License:* GNU Lesser General Public License *Contributors:* David Vignoni / ICON KING 23

Figure 11 *Source:* https//en.wikipedia.org *License:* Public Domain *Contributors:* Cornellrockey04, Docu, Frank C. Müller, Jwh, Krassotkin, Makthorpe, Man vyi, Mayyskiyysergeyy, Morio, Nobunaga24, Roo72, Zac Allan 24

Figure 12 *Source:* https://en.wikipedia.org/w/index.php?title=File:Ohrdruf_Corpses_Eisenhower.jpg *License:* Public Domain *Contributors:* Benchill, Catsmeat, Damian Yerrick, Docu, Giorgiomonteforti, Hohum, Mtsmallwood, Noclador, Pieter Kuiper, Sammyday, Slowking4, Sugarman, USHMM, Viciarg, WFinch, Zac Allan 27

Figure 13 *Source:* https://en.wikipedia.org/w/index.php?title=File:Patton_during_a_welcome_home_parade_in_Los_Angeles,_June_9,_1945.jpg *License:* Public Domain *Contributors:* Office of War Information 28

Figure 14 *Source:* https://en.wikipedia.org/w/index.php?title=File:General_Patton's_grave_300806.jpg *License:* Creative Commons Attribution-ShareAlike 3.0 Unported *Contributors:* BotMultichill, Jwh, Leyo, OgreBot 2, Rossrs~commonswiki, Väsk, 1 anonymous edits 30

Figure 15 *Source:* https://en.wikipedia.org/w/index.php?title=File:General_Patton_3c_1953_issue_U.S._stamp.jpg *License:* Public Domain *Contributors:* MrFrosty2 32

Figure 16 *Source:* https://en.wikipedia.org/w/index.php?title=File:Patton's_Command_Car.jpg *License:* Creative Commons Attribution 2.0 *Contributors:* Mike Fisher 33

Figure 17 *Source:* https://en.wikipedia.org/w/index.php?title=File:Patton's_.357_revolver.jpg *License:* Creative Commons Attribution-Sharealike 2.0 *Contributors:* cubby_t_bear 35

Figure 18 *Source:* https://en.wikipedia.org/w/index.php?title=File:Patton_Monument_West_Point_in_new_location_2009_upright.JPG *License:* Public Domain *Contributors:* Ahodges7 36

Figure 19 *Source:* https://en.wikipedia.org/w/index.php?title=File:2011-01-6_Baugnez_laarzen_van_George_Patton_6-01-2012_14-09-34.JPG *License:* Creative Commons Attribution-Sharealike 3.0,2.5,2.0,1.0 *Contributors:* Paul Hermans 38

Image *Source:* https://en.wikipedia.org/w/index.php?title=File:Cscr-featured.svg *License:* GNU Lesser General Public License *Contributors:* Anomie 41

Figure 20 *Source:* https://en.wikipedia.org/w/index.php?title=File:GeorgeSPatton.jpg *License:* Public Domain *Contributors:* Photo by U.S. Army Signal Corps 44

Figure 21 *Source:* https://en.wikipedia.org/w/index.php?title=File:Dwight_D_Eisenhower.jpg *License:* Public Domain *Contributors:* Unnamed photographer for US Army 48

Figure 22 *Source:* https://en.wikipedia.org/w/index.php?title=File:General_of_the_Army_Omar_Bradley.jpg *License:* Public Domain *Contributors:* GT1976, Harpsichord246, Hohum, Nobunaga24, Rklawton, Sciss~commonswiki, 1 anonymous edits 54

Image *Source:* https://en.wikipedia.org/w/index.php?title=File:Navy_Distinguished_Service_ribbon.svg *Contributors:* - 59

Image *Source:* https://en.wikipedia.org/w/index.php?title=File:Legion_of_Merit_ribbon.svg *Contributors:* AlanM1, EclecticArkie, EricSerge, FSII, FieldMarine, Flamurai, Huntster, Illegitimate Barrister, Ipankonin, Sarang, Sportsfan92 59

Image *Source:* https://en.wikipedia.org/w/index.php?title=File:Bronze_Star_Medal_ribbon.svg *Contributors:* Defense Logistics Agency 59

Image *Source:* https://en.wikipedia.org/w/index.php?title=File:Purple_Heart_ribbon.svg *Contributors:* AlanM1, Alno, Arch dude, CORNELIUSSEON, Ed!, FSII, FieldMarine, Illegitimate Barrister, Ipankonin, Jappalang, Jatkins, Juiced lemon, Madmedea, Magasjukur2, Mboro, Orem, Sarang 59

Image *Source:* https://en.wikipedia.org/w/index.php?title=File:Silver_Lifesaving_Medal_ribbon.svg *Contributors:* Ipankonin 59

Image *Source:* https://en.wikipedia.org/w/index.php?title=File:Mexican_Border_Service_Medal_ribbon.svg *Contributors:* Ipankonin 59

Image *Source:* https://en.wikipedia.org/w/index.php?title=File:American_Defense_Service_Medal_ribbon.svg *Contributors:* Ipankonin 59

Image *Source:* https://en.wikipedia.org/w/index.php?title=File:World_War_II_Victory_Medal_ribbon.svg *Contributors:* Ipankonin 59

Image *Source:* https://en.wikipedia.org/w/index.php?title=File:Army_of_Occupation_ribbon.svg *Contributors:* Ipankonin 59

Image *Source:* https://en.wikipedia.org/w/index.php?title=File:Grand_Officer_Ordre_de_Leopold.png *License:* Public Domain *Contributors:* Wiki Romi 59

Image *Source:* https://en.wikipedia.org/w/index.php?title=File:UK_MID_1920-94.svg *License:* Public Domain *Contributors:* Mboro 59

Image *Source:* https://en.wikipedia.org/w/index.php?title=File:Czechoslovak_War_Cross_1939-1945_Ribbon.png *License:* Creative Commons Attribution-Sharealike 3.0 *Contributors:* Dandvsp (talk) 60

Image *Source:* https://en.wikipedia.org/w/index.php?title=File:Legion_Honneur_GO_ribbon.svg *Contributors:* Orem (wiki-pl: Orem, commons: Orem) 60

Image *Source:* https://en.wikipedia.org/w/index.php?title=File:CroixdeGuerreFR-BronzeStar.png *License:* Creative Commons Attribution-Sharealike 3.0 *Contributors:* Jesmar, LuigiXIV, Sarang 60

Image *Source:* https://en.wikipedia.org/w/index.php?title=File:Croix_de_guerre_1939–1945_stripe_bronsepalme.svg *License:* Creative Commons Attribution-Sharealike 3.0 *Contributors:* User:Ordensherre 60

Image *Source:* https://en.wikipedia.org/w/index.php?title=File:French_Liberation_Medal_ribbon.png *License:* Public domain *Contributors:* Dandvsp 60

Image *Source:* https://en.wikipedia.org/w/index.php?title=File:LUX_Order_of_Adolphe_Nassau_Grand_Cross_BAR.png *License:* Creative Commons Attribution-Sharealike 3.0 *Contributors:* User:Mimich 60

Image *Source:* https://en.wikipedia.org/w/index.php?title=File:LUX_Croix_de_Guerre_ribbon.svg *License:* Public Domain *Contributors:* Mboro 60

Image *Source:* https://en.wikipedia.org/w/index.php?title=File:Ordre_de_l'Ouissam_Alaouite_GC_ribbon_(Maroc).svg *License:* Creative Commons Attribution 3.0 *Contributors:* Boroduntalk 60

Image *Source:* https://en.wikipedia.org/w/index.php?title=File:Order_kutuzov1_ribbon.jpg *License:* Creative Commons Attribution-Sharealike 3.0 *Contributors:* EHDI5YS (talk) 60

Image *Source:* https://en.wikipedia.org/w/index.php?title=File:Order_of_the_Bath_UK_ribbon.png *License:* Public Domain *Contributors:* Image sourced from 'Medals of the World' website: http://www.medals.org.uk/index.htm 60

Image *Source:* https://en.wikipedia.org/w/index.php?title=File:US-O2_insignia.svg *License:* Public Domain *Contributors:* Yaddah (talk) 61

Image *Source:* https://en.wikipedia.org/w/index.php?title=File:US-O3_insignia.svg *License:* Public Domain *Contributors:* Ipankonin 61

Image *Source:* https://en.wikipedia.org/w/index.php?title=File:US-O4_insignia.svg *License:* Public Domain *Contributors:* Ipankonin 61

License

Index

Second lieutenant, 5
Second Sino-Japanese War, 14
Seine, 21
Self-propelled artillery, 21
Sereno E. Brett, 11
Serrig, 26
Service summary of George S. Patton, **57**
Seventh United States Army, 2, 17, 41, 44, 65
Shell shock, 43, 45
Shreveport, Louisiana, 15
Sicily Campaign, 43
Siege of Bastogne, 3, 70
Siegfried Line, 22
Sierra Blanca, Texas, 8
Silver Lifesaving Medal, 60
Silver Star, 2, 60
Silver Star Medal, 23
Simon Bolivar Buckner Jr., 41
Simon & Schuster, 39
Smith & Wesson Model 27, 32, 65
Sodium amytal, 46
Soviet Union, 27
Speyer, 31
Spinal decompression, 31
Stackpole Books, 40
Staff officer, 13
Stars and Stripes (newspaper), 38
St Crispins Day Speech, 70
Stephen E. Ambrose, 39
Stephen McNally, 32
Steven Zaloga, 71
Stockholm, 3, 5, 6, 30
Suicide, 50
Supreme Allied Commander, 16, 53
Sweden, 3, 5
Swimming (sport), 7

Tandem Library Group, 40
Tank, 10
Tank Corps of the American Expeditionary
    Force, 3
Tank Corps of the American Expeditionary
    Forces, 11
Task Force Baum, 26
Tear gas, 13
Tennessee Maneuver Area, 15
Terry Brighton, 31, 39, 66, 71
Terry de la Mesa Allen Sr., 19
Theater (warfare), 53
The Big Picture (TV series), 41
The Last Days of Patton, 32
The Long Way Home (1997 film), 32
Theodore Roosevelt Jr., 19
The Saturday Evening Post, 67
Third Battle of Winchester, 6
Third United States Army, 54, 63

Thomas Beecham, 41
Track and field, 5
Trier, 26
True Confessions (magazine), 51
Tunis, 54
Tunisia Campaign, 2, 17, 45
Tuscaloosa, Alabama, 40
Twelfth United States Army Group, 21
Twenty First Army Group, 22

Ultra, 22
Ulysses S. Grant, 37
Unintentional discharge (firearms), 8
United Kingdom, 53, 63
United States Armed Forces, 14
United States Army, 1, 2, 5, 43, 57
United States Army Cavalry School, 13
United States Army Center of Military History,
    55, 56
United States Army Central, 2, 14, 41
United States Army Command and General
    Staff College, 11, 13
United States Army War College, 13, 58
United States Cavalry, 2, 5
United States Congress, 43
United States House of Representatives, 52
United States Military Academy, 2, 4, 61
United States Olympic Team, 57
United States Secretary of War, 6
United States Senate Committee on Armed
    Services, 52
United States Third Army, 63
University of Alabama Press, 40
University of North Carolina Press, 56
U.S. 101st Airborne Division, 25
U.S. 13th Cavalry Regiment, 9
U.S. 15th Army, 30
U.S. 17th Field Artillery Regiment, 47
U.S. 1st Infantry Division, 45
U.S. 26th Infantry Regiment, 46
U.S. 3rd Infantry Division, 50
U.S. 4th Armored Division, 22
U.S. 5th Cavalry Regiment, 14
U.S. 6th Armored Division, 66
U.S. 6th Infantry Regiment, 9
U.S. Army, 31
U.S. Army Air Forces, 25
U.S. Army Chief of Staff, 8
US First Lieutenant, 61
US General, 65
U.S. II Corps, 46, 65
U.S. III Corps, 25
US Lieutenant Colonel, 49
US Lieutenant General, 43
US Major, 47
US Major General, 45

91

www.ingramcontent.com/pod-product-compliance
Lightning Source LLC
Chambersburg PA
CBHW031538040426
42445CB00010B/594